REVERSAL

by

Eric Linne

CHAPTER ONE: DOWN THAT HOLE

The teacher drones out the names of students and halfhearted hands reach up to grab English papers. The first writing assignment of the year—"How I Spent my Summer Vacation." Do they still do that baby stuff in ninth grade? Really? Maybe here they do. I've got a lot to learn about this place. Finally, the moment I've been dreading.

"Burbridge... Kayla Burbridge?" Mr. Chenoweth asks imploringly.

"It's pronounced 'Burbadge.'" Twenty-eight sets of eyes from every corner of the classroom shoot at me in unison. Great. Just what I need at a new school in a new town—attention. Any attention. I look away from the curious eyes, peel open my paper and scan for my grade. Nothing. Just a scrawl across the top in fiery crimson marker: *"Please see me after school today."* Outstanding. Six days into a new school year and already I've pissed off a teacher. So much so that he won't grade my paper. This is exactly what I hoped for.

      I suppose I could have written that I spent the summer learning new and interesting skills. Skills like how to treat the hundreds of tiny cuts a girl gets each day when detasseling corn. Or mad skills like how to get glue-sticky hay out of your hair and ears after a day of pitching giant bales from a muddy field onto a clunky, rolling farm wagon on a ninety-six degree day. Such fun! Or the always useful skill of holding one's breath while cleaning years-old crusty cow crap out of a spider-filled barn. That's something every fourteen-year-old girl needs to know.

      I shouldn't complain about having summer jobs. *"Not in this economy,"* the Spurlings tell me. Not that I'm a girly girl, but all of that manual labor did a number on my nails. I wouldn't mind that if I could just get them back to normal. Something like the fun blueberry creme I had after my last trip to the Vietnamese salon on Argyle Street with her. It was our Saturday tradition. Hot chocolate and Swedish pancakes with lingonberries.

Then a brief stroll over to the salon. Not much, looking back on it. But it was our thing. Now it's gone.

Instead of writing what I was supposed to, I wrote what's on my mind every waking minute and what I dream about every night. I think where I went drastically wrong in my essay was in my conclusion. I made the mistake of describing how all of this makes me feel. It wasn't even part of the assignment! Rookie mistake. But now the cards are on the table. The bell rings. The other kids, who belong here, snag their backpacks and flee this prison for another one just like it. I avoid making eye contact with Mr. Chenoweth as I dart between two straggling girls and slink out the door. Don't worry Mr. C. As Arnold said, *"I'll be back."*

I have a theory that an elite club of sado-masochists meets once per month to ponder one important question. How can we make the lives of adolescent girls a living nightmare for forty-five minutes every day and brand it as education? Let's call it *physical* education. Brilliant. And they've been able to sell this particularly exquisite brand of cruelty to every freakin' high school in the country.

Of course, Felton High wouldn't want to rock the boat. That's where I live now—Felton, Indiana. A universe away from my former life.

So, after English class, I bumble my way through the inevitable indignity that we shorten to P.E. and say a silent prayer of thanks when the bell mercifully ends the class. I dutifully wet my hair just a tad in the sink to simulate a shower (school rules!) and wait in the most remote corner of the gym for the hallways to clear. When the jocks and jockettes file into the gym in groups of four or five in matching uniforms, that's my cue that it's safe to venture into the public spaces of the school.

I wander my way back to my English classroom. *She* would have called it "dilly dallying." Not in any hurry for what is about to happen. When I push open the creaky door, he looks up and smiles.

"Come in, Kayla. Have a seat…anywhere."

What's this all about? He doesn't seem angry at all. He seems…I don't know….almost nice.

"I wanted to talk to you about the writing

assignment. Do you feel up to that?"

Is he giving me a choice?

"Sure…I guess."

"Kayla, I'm really sorry. I didn't know anything about your…situation. I'm sorry if this exercise made you feel uncomfortable. I would have given another assignment."

This is not going so badly. I nod my head and glance up. He meets my eyes and gets more serious.

"I know this is difficult for you, but do you mind if I read a couple of parts of your paper to you?"

Gulp, now it's heading downhill. I nod again and hand my essay over.

"OK. You start with 'Why in the world would I want to write about this place? I hate it here. Here's why.'"

He stops abruptly and glances up from my paper. His face gets all serious, the way adults do when they are about to drop some bad news on you.

"I understand that you would be angry. With…with everything that's happened. Do you feel like talking about it?"

Keep my head down as I shake "no." My hair falls in my face. I like it there.

"Kayla, I think you need to talk to somebody about how you're feeling. Do you have anybody here? Maybe a pastor?"

Shake my head no—fast—as I memorize the desk, carved deeply with the initials JD. I sure don't have a pastor here.

"OK, but I think you should speak to the school guidance counselor about... about where you are."

Keep my eyes on the desk. Mostly thinking that a kid couldn't have carved those initials with a pen. They are about a half-inch deep. So, some kid, I guess named JD, brought a knife to school. And some teacher let him carve up the desk for a long time. What is wrong with this place?

"Kayla, she's had a lot of experience helping kids like you."

Flash of red behind my eyes and I hear myself screaming. "She doesn't know anything about me!" *Did I just say that?*

"Of course not, but she can get to know

you—and what you've been through."

I look up after what seems like hours. Stare at him through my hair and sit…and sit. I can do this all day.

"Kayla, she's really nice. She cares about the kids. All of them. Even the…all of them."

I let my stare break down. I'm not this girl. I know who I used to be. No more.

"I need to get home. I've got chores and …Junior."

Now it's his turn to stare back at me. He doesn't look mad or anything. I think he looks kind of…sad? I just want to leave. My heart is beating fast, my face is hot and my stomach feels weird. Mr. Chenoweth waits – just waits, saying nothing.

"OK," I say. "I'll meet her. But she's not going to fix anything."

"Great. I'll set it up for you. And by the way, your essay was very well written. You're a skilled writer. And I love that you read all those books over the summer."

"Can I leave now?"

"See you tomorrow."

I bolt out of the chair and head for the door.

"Kayla, I know it doesn't seem like it now. But things will get better."

Right. That's easy for you to say. Walk away fast, not looking back. Disaster averted. For now.

CHAPTER TWO: HER SAUCER OF MILK AT TEA-TIME

Safely out of Chenoweth's interrogation, I meander through the halls, passing the janitor mopping the hallway. I didn't realize they had any black people here. He smiles and nods as I pass by. Give him a little wave and half smile back. Push my way out the creaking, heavy double doors of the school. Taking my time, wandering the short distance to the two bike racks perched forlornly at a dismal corner littered with fast food trash, where the parking lot ends and a cornfield begins. At the far end of the parking lot, a large boy stands alone, staring in my direction. My eyes sweep the ground to avoid contact with him. I unlock my springy silver bike cable ($6.99 at Wal-Mart, after price rollback) and bump out my brown girls' Schwinn Varsity, 1970s-vintage, 10-speed bike (reduced to $25 at Goodwill). I zigzag my way through the parking lot, look both ways, and turn right on East

Street, followed by a quick left on Washington Street. No cars and no people walking. I'm not in Chicago anymore. Not even close.

If school is like a prison with walls, then my home life here is more of a work release program. I'm working off my debt to society. Not sure what my crime was, but I feel like I'm an indentured servant. I'd like to keep riding past home, sit by that teeny roadside creek I found the other day and start rereading *Alice's Adventures in Wonderland*. It's peaceful there and I can be alone. Just me and Alice—again. But June instructed me to: "…git right home after school, feed those dogs and keep an eye on Arvin Jr." So I'm rolling on home. Not stopping, not dawdling, but damn sure not peddling my fastest.

I hate those evil things. The "hounds of hell" is my private name for them. Arvin calls them something weird like "Tige" and "Prince." But it's fun coming up with new names for their peculiar brand of malevolence. Yesterday, I called them "Mad Dog" and "Rabies." Fair descriptions. Today, I'm going with "Beelzebub" and "Beetlejuice." That feels just right. Not that those drooling, snapping, nasty hound dogs care what I call them, as long as they get their food. I'm sure they would devour me without a second thought if they could break those thick chains that bind them to their smelly dog houses. When I struggle pulling their economy-size feed bag from the shed, each dog bolts to the end of its chain and strains against its choke collar like a fox struggling futilely to pull its leg out of a trap. These hounds don't seem to mind the self-inflicted pain. They only want to get at the food, then get at me, then devour any living thing they can get their slimy jaws around. They live to eat, nothing more or less.

  I pull the rake behind me, the tines catching in the overgrown grass. June tells me it's a bow rake. That's a useful tidbit of knowledge that I didn't have (or need) six months ago. As the hounds howl furiously just out of my reach, I extend the rake out to grab their bowls and drag them away from their decrepit wooden houses over to my side. A little dark form creeps slowly into my field of vision. It stops. Stepping slowly, stealthily, on my right side. A nine-year-old, skinny boy dressed in faded blue overalls, no shirt, with filthy shoeless feet, bursts in front of me, waving a soup bone, just out of reach of the dogs.

"Junior, get that bone out of here," I say. "You're making them crazy…well, crazier than normal."

He strikes a defiant stance and glares at me: "You're not my mom. And not the boss of me either."

"I'm the boss of you until June and Arvin get home. Then you're their problem. Get away from here—now!"

The boy turns and heads for the house. After a couple of steps, he spins back around, smiling, and throws the bone toward the dogs, just missing the top of my head. The darker dog gets to the bone first, backs away from the other and growls menacingly. The lighter dog stalks the darker one and lunges at it from three feet way. Teeth snap, chains crackle and the terrible growling reminds me of noises I heard once in a werewolf movie. After several seconds of the bedlam, the lighter dog sinks its teeth into the other's neck. With a horrible howl of pain, the darker dog drops the bone. The biter picks it up and marches victoriously back to its house. It devours the bone in seconds.

"Look what you did," I yell. "Now your dad is going to have to pay a vet."

"He ain't paying no vet. Those stupid dogs bite each other all the time."

"I don't care. Get in the house and do your homework."

"I ain't got no homework. I'm only in fourth grade, dummy."

"You don't have *any* homework."

He sneers, "I ain't got *any* homework."

I sigh and shake my head. "Junior, just get in the house and watch TV or something. Don't make me tell your mom again."

After I play the "mom" card, we stare at each other like two gunfighters in an old Western. After a few seconds, Junior takes two steps backward, toward the house. He jerks his right hand up abruptly and extends his middle finger—thrusting skyward three times. Turns and runs giggling into the house.

As the back door slams, two young girls walk up the drive. The older girl walks purposefully, staring straight ahead, while the younger one skips up the drive, shyly smiling in my direction.

"Hi Denise," I say. Then to the little one, "Hey, little sweetie."

The older girl ignores my greeting. Ignoring me is an improvement. Usually she asks me why I don't go back where I came from. She grabs her sister's hand and yanks her roughly toward the house. The little one looks over her shoulder, smiles and crinkles her fingers toward me. I wave back.

"Bye, Geneva," I say, more to myself than her.

Still haven't fed the dogs. At least one of them hasn't eaten anything. My only real chore tonight—shocking. I fill their industrial strength metal food bowls to overflowing and set them at my feet. The dogs eye me menacingly, like the Lincoln Park Zoo lions at feeding time. I shove their bowls, one at a time, just within their reach. The dark dog bolts toward me, biting the wood on my rake, just above the tines. I shake the rake a couple of times to loosen his grip. The hound lets go and attacks his food, devouring the chow as if he hadn't eaten in days. I push the other dog's bowl in, turn and drag the rake and feed bag back to the shed.

As I close the creaking shed door, a rusted, burnt red pickup truck pulls into the driveway slowly, crunching gravel until it rolls to a stop. It coughs, sputters, then silence. A man steps down from the truck carrying a gray, old-fashioned lunch pail. His lined face is streaked with dirt and sweat. He could be thirty-five or fifty-five years old. I happen to know that he's forty-five, but that's cheating.

"Hi Arvin."

"Oh, hey girl. How you doin?" He attempts a smile, but it's forced.

"Fine," I lie.

"Did you get them dogs fed?" He stretches and lazily rubs his lower back, grimacing.

"Yeah. I just fed them."

"Is supper ready?" He yawns and stretches his neck. "I am bone tired."

"June's not home yet."

"Not home? Well, girl, can you start gettin' something fixed? I got to get to bed early."

He turns away, without waiting for my reply. Heads toward the back door—a slight limp in his step. As if remembering something, he turns and looks at me. Studies my face for a while, then pulls off his lime green John Deere baseball cap and runs his fingers through his thinning hair.

"Girl, what's the matter?"

"Nothing."

"C'mon, now."

"It's just...why does Denise hate me so much?"

"She don't hate you, she's just..." He pauses and searches for words. The right ones. "It's just that Denise got used to bein' the only child. Got all her Momma's attention. Then Junior come along and then Geneva. But Denise was still the big girl of the family. He hesitates again—a good five seconds. "Then you come along."

"I didn't ask for..."

He cuts me off. "I know you didn't. But you're here anyway. Just give Denise some time. OK?"

What else am I going to do? "OK," I mutter.

"How 'bout that supper?" he asks.

Of course I can get something *fixed*. I don't have anything else to do. No homework, no books to read, no friends to call. Wait, that last part is true. Nobody—at least not in this town. Not a soul to call, or text, or IM or hang out with or laugh over nothing with. I'm alone here. Just me, myself and I. I brush a tear from my cheek, blow out my breath and clomp up the back steps. The screen door slams my behind, launching me into my next task.

CHAPTER THREE: WAKE UP, ALICE DEAR

I'm drifting...now floating...now flying. Higher and higher. I see the clouds... fluffy, puffy, blow them with my breath, all huffy. I want to fly over the clouds. I can do it. Oooooo, so soft. Pink clouds ahead. I float over them, thicker and stuffier than the rest. My nose crinkles and wrinkles from the sticky sweet smell.

Cotton candy! I want some! Reach my hand down into the cloud to grab a big bite. I can pull off a chunk, all frosty and delicious. A hand grabs me. Pulling me down. Noooooo! I want to fly. I want my clouds. I want my candy. Nooooooo! I don't want to go down!

"Kayla sweetheart, wake up." It's Mommy and she's holding my hand with hers—soft like my heart feels with her. Mommy would never pull me down. She's always right here. With me. "Hey, sleepyhead. Did you forget what day it is?"

"Is it my 6th Birthday?"

"No silly, it's Easter Sunday. Come downstairs and see if the Easter Bunny remembered you this year. Daddy's making chocolate chip pancakes."

I run downstairs to Daddy and crush him with a grizzly bear hug.

"Whoa there, Speedy Gonzales." Daddy says with his best movie star voice.

"Silly Daddy. I..am..the...ROADRUNNER today!"

"Right Missy, I knew that. Run and see what the Easter Bunny brought you."

"My Easter basket! He remembered me!" First the shiny pink paper I can see through. The rainbow is following me! Crinkly, squeaky green, green grass hiding everything I love. Chocolate bunnies, mushy peeps, a Kinder Surprise, a tiny box of Fanny May Trinidads (THE BEST), Easter eggs with jelly beans. All for me. A real Easter egg with a "Kayla" on it. That's for Daddy later. And at the bottom of the basket, a fluffly yellow stuffed bunny.

"My bunny!" I squeal. The most beautiful softest, smiley, love-happy stuffed bunny in the whole world. "Mommy, Daddy, I love him! He's *my best thing ever! I name him Bun-Bun. Oh, Bun-Bun. You will be my best friend. Always. Me and you together. I'll tell you every secret. Aaaaand you will make my dreams come true."*

"You'll be safe here," I tell Bun-Bun. "You'll always be safe. You listen to my secrets and I keep you safe. Mommy and Daddy keep me safe. We're safe and together...always and forever."

But, they aren't here. Only tangled sheets and my pillow—streaked with tears. Not again. Back in my room. My new room. The room Arvin and some buddies put together out of the Spurling's former attic. The ten-foot by twelve-foot room has unpainted plywood floors and whitewashed walls, which still give off the acrid woody smell of the town lumber mill. The center half of the floor has a clean beige carpet remnant donated by the Felton Baptist Church, where my new family have been long-time members.

The ceiling slants on two sides at a forty-five degree angle before meeting the side walls of fiberboard which rise less than five feet. When I move around my room, I can only stand upright in the middle third, even though I'm only five feet four. The remaining space requires a slight stoop. A single, glass globe ceiling light glaringly lights the room. I usually keep it off and use my desk lamp, an electric camping lantern which I can move around. I've got my old headlamp for reading in bed.

Most of the scant furniture in the room was scavenged from Grandma Avis' barn and shows signs of many years of wear and tear. The single bed wedged under the eave on the east wall is unpainted iron, on which burnt orange rust patches suggest an exotic Polynesian archipelago. The mattress, purchased from the Goodwill store in Sheffield, is reasonably firm and comfortable. I think it's bedbug free. Fingers' crossed! Scattered over my tangled bed are seven hard-cover books borrowed from the Shelby County Library. *The Great Gatsby, The Wizard of Oz* and my beloved *Alice*. The book I was reading *then*. The only other thing on the bed is my best friend, a frayed, yellowish, stuffed bunny. I call him Bun-Bun. We go back a long way.

My small oak desk had a previous life as a

child's school desk. According to Arvin, Grandma Avis bought it at an auction after the Black Rock School finally closed its doors in 1968. On the side of the desk, sits an old radio on which I try every night (unsuccessfully) to find music from WXRT in Chicago. The desk is centered on a small window at the far end of the room. From the window I can see the scant comings and goings of Porter Street at the southern end of the village. If I crane my neck to the right of the window, I can see the freight train which rumbles by the house four times daily, gently shaking the attic room like a tiny earthquake.

    In the bottom drawer of my desk is a padlocked, lacquered box I built in a class at the Lill Street Gallery in Chicago. All by myself, thank you. Inside the box, amid numerous newspaper articles, some written by Mom and others written about Dad, I've buried my favorite possessions. Deep within the box, below a false bottom, lie my treasures. The first, a man's ruby ring, was passed down from father to son in Dad's family. It's mine now. The box also contains a necklace which was created from Mom's grandmother's nursing school pin. Mom's most prized possession, now mine. At the bottom of the box rest thirteen glass prisms of various sizes. On May sixth of every year of my life, a new prism has appeared among my stash of birthday presents. Not this year, though.

On three of the plain white walls, I've hung posters to make the room a little less drab. On the side wall over my bed hangs a poster of John Lennon, his tiny sunglasses and white New York City T-shirt displaying an air of urban sophistication. Seems pretty foreign in this little farm town. On the other side wall, a poster of Dad. You know, that famous actor John Burbadge. He's in pioneer clothing for his most famous movie role in the film *The Fire Bear*. He watches over me while I sleep. On the end wall, opposite the window, above my miniature chest of drawers, hangs a brilliantly colored, nearly surreal poster depicting Alice staring in amazement at the wonderland of sights which surround her.

While the attic room contains no closet, my meager clothes hang by unmatched hangers from a metal clothes rack donated by a friend of the family who works for the local Goodwill store. My clothes consist of three pairs of generic jeans and eight tops in a thin range of muted colors, mostly blue. School colors! They hang forlornly from the single aluminum bar. Above the lonely clothes rack, Alice's electric blue dress, the blazing purple jacket of the Mad Hatter, the crushed velvet red waist coat of the March Hare and the otherworldly orange of the sage caterpillar provide a stark contrast to the bleakness of my wardrobe.

Roll out of bed. I'm already dressed. Fell asleep reading -- again.

"Kayla!" It's June. "Hurry up or you're gonna be late for school."

"Coming!" I pick up the six-foot aluminum pole and hook it into the stairs like Arvin showed me. Push down and out. Voila! I have my own private collapsible staircase. Carry my pole down and shove the stairs back into the ceiling. Or rather, the floor of my room. Hustle down the hallway and take the main stairs three at a time. Spin around the corner and into the kitchen. Deserted.

"Where are the kids?"

June pokes her head out from the pantry. "I sent them ahead on the bus. Arvin took Geneva to the sitter's on his way to work. Hurry up and get you some breakfast."

No time. I grab a handful of cereal and fling my backpack over my shoulder.

"Bye, June." I'm out the back door and headed for my bike when she calls out for me.

"You forgot your lunch." She tosses the brown paper bag in my direction and it arcs lazily in my direction. At the last possible moment, I reach up and snatch it mid-air.

"Maybe I'll try out for the baseball team."

June snorts out a laugh and waves goodbye. I grab my bike from under the plastic breezeway, aim it north and head off for another thrilling day at dear old Felton High. I sing McCartney's *Just Another Day* to make the dream go away.

CHAPTER FOUR: THE MEN ON THE CHESS BOARD

I think I've found a safe place to eat lunch. It only took me three weeks. Three long weeks of ridicule, rejection, and too many food bombs to count. For the time being, I will be dining in the friendly confines of the school's baseball field bleachers. Front row!

Since baseball practice starts in the spring, I've got the place to myself. Except for the girl with the crutches on the far side of the bleachers, a few rows behind me. She looks up from her book and nods, then checks me out for a while. I dig into my bag for today's dining delicacies. Ugh. Another bologna sandwich. I need to start packing my own lunch. Which means that I need to get up earlier. Which means that I need to set my own alarm. Which means…

"So who kicked you out?" she asks. "Wait, don't tell me. Let me guess."

"I didn't get kicked…"

"Was it the Ag Kids? No, I don't see you as the overall wearing type. The Artsies? Couldn't be. Their table is already too small for the three of them. You look smarter than to hang out with the Future Methies of America."

I shake my head, and she gives me a knowing smile.

"You're too small to be a jock girl. And there isn't room at the God Squad table. Their numbers are growing exponentially."

I try to respond but she cuts me off. "Oh God, you didn't try to sit with Madison, Raven and the Sheffield Wannabees? That would be social suicide."

"My name's Kayla," I say. "What's yours?"

"It's Kenna Faye." She methodically and slowly makes her way down the three rows of bleachers and slides into the seat behind me. She carefully hooks her crutches on the dusty silver seat by the arm supports.

I extend my hand. "Nice to meet you, Kenna."

She grips mine with a firm hand—stronger

than I expected.

"It's Kenna *Faye*."

"Right. Sorry. Kenna Faye."

She smiles crookedly and winks. "That's OK. I get that all the time."

I open my sandwich and peer in—expecting it to have morphed into something edible. I peel the thick bologna slice off and toss it behind me. It snags on a bleacher railing. We both stare and then simultaneously burst into laughter.

"At least it's Gray's bread," I say. "Not some white Wonder bread crap."

"Did you get that in Sheffield?"

"No. The woman who takes care of me works at the bakery. She brings home stuff from there all the time. It's the only decent food I've had since moving here."

"The woman who…?"

"Well, she's not really my step-Mom, so I don't know what to call her."

Kenna Faye gazes with amusement, as though I'm telling a fascinating story.

"The woman's husband is my Dad's cousin. Was my Dad's cousin." I stop and take a long pull from my water bottle. "So I don't really know what I am to all of them."

"Sounds complicated."

"I guess. Actually, you're the first person here who's asked anything about me. Thanks for that."

"Don't mention it."

We eat in silence for a moment. Enjoying the sunny, breezy fall day. I close my eyes and turn my face to the sun for a full minute.

"Oh crap," she says. "Here they come."

I turn my face away from the sun as two tall boys stride from the pitcher's mound toward us. Both have their shirts pulled up and tied, exposing muscled stomachs. Each boy has a felt marker hanging by a string around his neck.

The blond boy saunters up and parks himself immediately in front of me. "Looks like we got ourselves a croaker here."

His buddy joins in. "Yep. Looks like you snagged yourself a live one."

Kenna Faye snarls, "Why don't you guys go bother somebody else?"

Blondie sneers. "Cause I caught myself a

livin', breathin' froggy, right here. If it's any of your business, limpy."

Kenna Faye grabs one of her crutches and slowly pulls herself to her feet. "Maybe I'll make it my business, Donnie."

Donnie's friend interrupts, "We're just having a little fun with the frog."

I glance up at the boys, then turn to Kenna Faye. "Are they talking about me?"

She nods her head.

"I'm not a frog," I say.

"Not a frog? I heard otherwise."

Kenna Faye looks disgusted. "A frog is what these juveniles call a freshman."

Donnie nods. "See, she understands how it works." He slowly and dramatically unwinds the pen from his neck, stares at it a few seconds and drops it at my feet.

"Well frog, pick it up and do your thing."

"First of all, I'm not your frog. And…"

"OK, *freshman*. Pick up the pen and go to work."

I stare at the boy, motionless.

Donnie says, "Would somebody please

explain to her how it works?"

I tear away from his gaze and glance back at Kenna Faye. She shakes her head and says, "It's their stupid fraternity initiation. He wants you to pick up the pen and sign his stomach."

"Yeah, sign his rock hard abs," Donnie's friend chimes in.

I smile for a second, then it falls away. These guys are actually serious. I stand and start to collect my lunch trash. I've dealt with bullies before. I'm from Chicago.

"Well? I haven't got all day," Donnie says

"Oh?" I drop the pack on the seat and stare up at him, about ten inches over my head. "I'm not playing your little game."

Donnie stares for a few seconds in disbelief. Then he reaches down and whips his pen off the ground. "Let's beat it, Todd. Leave these lesbo losers to their miserable selves."

Todd sneers in our direction and turns wordlessly to follow his friend, already five steps ahead of him on the diamond.

"Always a pleasure, Todd and Donnie," Kenna Faye sings out.

Donnie takes a quarter turn toward us and grabs his crotch. "Bite me!"

"Oh no, Donnie," says Kenna Faye. "Remember, you've got a girlfriend."

The boys walk away, pretending not to hear.

"Sorry you had to go through that idiocy," Kenna Faye consoles.

"That's OK. But why didn't they try to get you to sign?"

"Me? Are you kidding? I'm not a damn frog." Kenna Faye stares for two beats then breaks into giggles. I join in.

"I went through it last year. I'm a big sophomore now. Woo hoo."

I nod.

"But seriously, you've got to get hooked up with a group. You know, a posse, a social network, some buds, bros, hombres, homies…friends?"

"I wasn't exactly thinking about this place long term."

"Well, you better think short term. Winter can be bit harsh here in the stands."

"I know." A little whiny. I can hear my

own voice.

"And you don't want to end up with the kids who don't eat lunch. Hanging out in the gym."

"Why don't they eat lunch?"

"Lots of reasons. No money. No food in the house. No parents in the house." She pauses and gets serious. "Bad parents in the house. Or maybe some of them are dieting. I don't know."

I smile and Kenna Faye returns it. "It's almost bell time." She slings her pack over her shoulder and walks awkwardly toward the gym. "It's been a slice of heaven."

I toss my trash toward the can and nail it from eight feet. "She shoots, she scores!"

Kenna Faye turns and smiles in my direction. She waves gently with the crutch dangling from her right arm. I brush the dust off my butt and lope back to the grind.

CHAPTER FIVE: THE DUCHESS AND THE COOK

"Another day, another dollar."

That's what Mr. Pawlesky, our neighbor in Chicago, said every morning as he got into his car to go to work. As a kid, I always thought it was weird that he was so excited about earning one dollar a day. Now I get it. He probably meant that one day is pretty much just like every other day. I'm beginning to understand what he meant. I point my bike out of the driveway and onto Porter Street. Headed to school, but I don't need to take the direct route. I've got time for a little exploring. Time to catch a few of the sights in Felton. My bike seat is cold and hard. I have to leave it under the porch at night. Can't wait to see what it feels like in January. June says I need to "Stop complaining," and "Toughen up." I already feel like I've toughened up since last April. Not sure how much tougher I can get.

I swerve onto Main Street and head north. No traffic on the road except a combine. Five months ago, I didn't even know what a combine was. Now I can tell that the one creeping along up ahead is an International Harvester. Not bad for a city girl. Former city girl, I should say. The tractor is bright red, with three IU stickers in the back window. That is one Hoosier-lovin' farmer. What else is there to do here besides follow sports? I didn't have much to do with sports in my former life. Now I know that the Hoosiers and some team called the Boilers are locked in heated, seemingly endless battles. Oh man…what some people choose to waste their time on.

Two blocks north on Main, I turn right onto the most exciting boulevard in Felton—Washington Street. Their version of the Mag Mile. Riiight.

I push the hair out of my eyes and pick out my favorite landmarks. There's Molly's Video Store and Tanning Emporium. Guess they haven't gotten the word of Blockbuster's demise yet. And the tanning thing? Didn't that go out in like the 1980s? Old habits die hard in some places. I pedal on and spot the combination burger joint and pool hall. A couple of older boys stare out the window as I ride by. The muscular blond with the kinky hair blows a kiss my way. His buddy laughs hysterically and drops his pool stick, bending over in his mirth. As I glance back, his friend pushes him over and swipes the quarters off the pool table. I'm sure that little exchange will end well.

I pass the main intersection and pedal the final two blocks to school. Past the professional part of town. First, the tiny Farmer's Bank branch in an understated, elegant building. At least, it's elegant by Felton standards. A lawyer's office next. Deserted at this hour, he seems to do most of his business at night. The two-room free health clinic shares space with the town vet. I'm sure she's not in now either—likely out at one of the farms birthing a cow or horse or something. I saw that happen last summer. Arvin made me watch. Said I would never see that in the big city. He's right about that. The milking barn at Lincoln Park Zoo is the closest I've gotten to the business end of a cow. At first, I thought I was going to get sick. But the mother cow locked eyes with me and would not look away. Gave birth to her baby without making a sound. I never told anyone, but it was kind of cool. Maybe I'll be a vet someday. Got to get through the fall semester of ninth grade first.

Almost to school and I pass Black Rock Hardwoods. I've peeked in the windows before. A middle-aged, red-haired lady sanding away on furniture in the back room. A front showroom full of samples. Looks like nice stuff. Furniture like I've seen in my parents' trendy friends' houses in Chicago. As I ride by, she is sitting in a gorgeous oak rocker in front of her store. Is that what I think it is? Does she have a cup of Starbucks? Where would she get that around here? She must have seen me staring because she waves. I nod back at her and bear down with my left foot to gain some speed. The school parking lot looms ahead and there is a backup of three cars waiting to turn in. That's what they call a Felton, Indiana traffic jam. I turn left on East Street and head for the back of the school. Sometimes I like to lock my bike around a tree near the dumpsters. Less contact with the locals. Today I can slip in the side entrance and walk just a few feet to my first class—Government with Mr. Monger.

As I pass through the doorway, the usual pre-class bedlam ensues. Why do boys always think that they can impress girls by acting like doofuses (or is that doofi)? Not sure why, but it seems to work around here. The girls can't get enough of some kid trying to stuff two egg and bacon sandwiches into his mouth at once. Really appetizing to watch. I look away and push my way through two girls to get to the last row -- my usual haven. As I sit and reach into my backpack, I see two figures hovering on either side of me.

"Hey there, I'm Madison," the blond girl points just above her cleavage. "And this is Raven." She points to the other girl, tall and thin with the blackest dyed hair I've ever seen. "Say hey, Raven."

The dye job girl flutters her fingers at me and says, "Hey, Raven." Then laughs hysterically at her own lame joke.

"And your name is Kylie?" Madison asks, breaking into her best down-home smile. Way too much lipstick and makeup.

"It's Kayla." I hesitate. "Hi?"

"Where ya from Kyla?"

It's Kayla, moron. What's the point? "I'm from Chicago. Was from there. Now I live here." Duh, now I sound like the moron.

"Oh. I had a friend who went there once. She said it was dirty and noisy. But the shops are to die for," Madison coos, twirling her hair.

"It's not so bad," I say. "Most tourists never see any of the city beyond the Loop. It's a nice place to live."

"Whatever." She reaches into her too-tight jeans and pulls out a small package. Smiles at her friend Raven, who returns her smile.

"You want some gum?" Madison pushes a stick out of the full pack and waves it at me.

"No, thanks."

She frowns and takes a step back. "It's OK." She brightens. "It's sugar free." Raven nods her head emphatically in agreement.

To get them out of here I reach for one and pop it into my mouth as the teacher walks in, closing the door behind him. Raven and Madison twirl around and move toward their seats near the front. As she passes the teacher's desk, Madison throws the remainder of the pack of gum discreetly into the trash can.

"Get out some paper," Monger monotones. "We're starting with a pop quiz." About twenty kids in the class groan in unison.

"Quiet! First question..." Madison's hand shoots up. "What is it, Miss Bell?"

"Did you change the rule about gum in your classroom?"

"I most certainly didn't. Why do you ask?"

"Well, I just thought maybe I missed it. Because the new girl...she has..."

Raven blurts, "She's chewing gum."

I stop mid-chew and stare blankly first at Raven, then Madison. Raven stares back vacantly. No one home. But Madison shows the tiniest hint of a smirk, her head behind Mr. Monger's glare. I glance up like a deer in the headlights. Pinned. Can't ...look...away.

"Miss Burbadge?" Nothing from me. Can I swallow it? It'll never work.

"Yes?"

"Well, *are* you chewing gum?"

"I...they..." I stare intently at my sneakers. Geneva colored a little picture of a flower on the left toe with her red pen last night. I don't mind. "Yes, sir. Sorry, sir." Might as well lay it on thick.

"Please spit it out. Now!" He points his bony finger at the trash can like Ichabod Crane pointing at the horseman.

I march to the front of the room—not acknowledging stares from the entire class. Snickers erupt from multiple parts of the room.

"Silence!" Monger bellows. "Since you're new here, Mizz Burbadge, let me tell you how it works. That is your first and second strike. No more warnings. Next infraction lands you in detention."

I swallow my tears and stare down. Please God, let me die right now. I'm feeling sick again. Monger mercifully continues with the quiz and then lectures on about the separation of powers in the U.S. Not sure he's getting through to most of them.

When class ends, Madison and Raven grab the arms of a classmate and scream laughter into both her ears. The girl covers her ears, but laughs along with them as they squeeze through the doorway. I grab my bag and stamp out the door after them. My face burns and the sick feeling in my stomach is just a knot now. They are half a hall ahead of me, picking up members of their entourage along the way. Madison spins gracefully to her right and leans against a locker.

I pick up speed and nearly knock down a small boy who warns, "Hey screwball, watch it!"

"Sorry," I mumble and bear down on Madison, now surrounded by a fawning posse of five girls.

I push myself into the center or her group. Madison looks up and smiles. She's in her element.

"What was that stunt you pulled back there?" *Stunt? Really?* I sound like Mom. My Mom.

"What do you mean?" She flashes her brightest smile. I'm sure it always works on the Felton boys. Flips her hair.

"You know damn well what I mean. Why me? What did I ever do to you?"

"You messed with Donnie and I…"

"Who the hell is Donnie?" Her posse roars with laughter, but Madison plays it cool.

"Now who's Donnie? Who's Donnie? Just the best basketball player in the school. And on the student counsel. And the hottest guy in the Junior class." She pauses for emphasis. Makes sure I'm listening, so she leans in. "He's also my boyfriend...and you and your little twerp friend messed with him."

I stare at her perplexed. I have no idea what she's talking about. It must show in my expression. Poor dumb new girl.

"You can't really be that dense. The guys at the baseball field? The frat initiation? Ring a bell, Kylie?"

"It's Kayla! And if you ever..." I drop my bag and get in her face. Up close. Her pack of girls takes a step back, but closes the circle. My hand clenches into a fist. I have no idea what I'm about to do. Then a strong hand grabs my shoulder and gently spins me a quarter turn. His other arm snags my pack and he steers me away from Madison's gang and toward the gym. I hear a mix of laughter and squealing in the background. I start to turn, but he holds tight to my arm.

"Are you OK?" I look up and see the big boy. The one who watched me from the parking lot.

"What? You're the…"

"I'm Hollis." He sticks out his meaty paw and I take it. Like a child shaking hands with a giant.

"You're new here. You don't want to get messed up with those people."

"I don't need anybody rescuing me. I can take care of myself, thank you."

"I'm sure you can. Just don't want to see you get started like that. It's…"

I ignore him and take two steps toward the gym to get away. I know the gym. It's safe.

Hollis moves quickly between me and the gym door. Pretty fast for a big guy. He blocks my way.

"You don't want to go in there now. *They* are in there. 'Holding court' they call it. You need to learn your way around here."

"Who's in there …and what's this 'court'?"

"It's Sperry and Dole. A couple of bad dudes. Stay as far away from them as you can. I'm serious, Kayla." *How does he know my name? How do they all seem to know my name? Except Madison, that is.*

I let out my breath, turn and walk away from the gym—toward my locker. Hollis hands me my bag and follows five feet behind me. I gather my things for the night and the giant silently escorts me to my bike. As I ride away, I take one look back. He's still there watching and waves slowly. I give a small nod and pedal into the fall afternoon.

CHAPTER SIX: YOU'RE NOTHING BUT A PACK

The class bell jangles overhead and students begin to spill into the cramped halls. Kids push their way through the crowds, some shouting at friends, others clearing a space with elbows to pry open their lockers. The younger students cling to the walls, not venturing into the senior-dominated mosh pit which the center of the hallway has become.

I creep my way along the wall and head toward that unrequested appointment with the guidance counselor, who waits in a sparse office deep in the bowels of the administrative suite. I hang back, hugging the corner where two halls intersect. Trying to resist being swept downstream as the hoard of students makes its way through the stuffy, grim, poorly-lit halls. Most are dressed in simple attire—ripped dirty jeans, overalls, T-shirts with '80s hair bands splashed across the front, cowboy boots, mud-caked work boots and an abundance of baseball hats bearing the names of tractors, trucks and farm implement companies. My clothes are a swirl of blues in various shades, like clashing hues in a paint store color wheel. Sky blue, off-brand sneakers with Velcro straps, a navy blue V-neck tee one size too large and faded. Nearly white blue jeans which recently hung from the rack of a Sheffield Goodwill store. I wear the blues to try to blend in with the school spirit geeks in their Felton Mohawk sweatshirts and T-shirts. It's not working. Leaning into the wall, I try to become invisible in its cold embrace. That's not working either.

Two boys push at each other ten feet away down the hall. A tiny clearing develops around the boys as students jostle to either side to avoid the impending scuffle. A teacher lifts her head above the crowd, spots the struggling students. Immediately, she turns on her heel, walking slowly in the other direction. Friends of the boys pull them apart and they stalk off in opposite directions—a fight postponed till another time.

I hold my position on the corner and wait for the crowds to disperse. Not that I'm in any hurry to see the counselor. Hesitating just beside a large glass case, memorializing the scant athletic accomplishments of Felton Senior High School through the ages. The crowd thins when the warning bell sounds. I step to the middle of the six-feet-high by eight-feet-wide smudged glass case and study the contents. Most of the trophies, ribbons and other awards are old and tarnished. Graying, wrinkled pictures of runners and basketball players dot the corners of the case, some capturing action and some showing rows of farm boys, staring dully toward the camera, sporting their antique athletic uniforms.

The center third of the glass case houses an enormous gleaming gold trophy. Squinting at the trophy inscription, I make out: *2004 State Division 1-A Volleyball Champions – Felton Warriors*. Beneath the trophy is a massive, professionally shot photograph of a smiling girls' volleyball team. Two girls in the center of the picture hold the oversized trophy aloft. Glancing quickly at the picture, I find myself doing a double take. The girls are twins—identical twins. The caption under the picture reads: *Amanda and Amy Carlson proudly display*

Felton's first state championship trophy. Who knew?

I avoid looking up as a small group of students approaches. Late for class, but not hurrying. As they walk within six feet of me, one of the girls laughs breezily, and I catch a few words of their hushed conversation. It's Madison and Raven. Great. I glance up and see Donnie and Todd, my new friends from the baseball field. It just keeps getting better. After the classroom incident, I make it a point to study the girls. They are attractive. I mean attractive by Felton standards. Madison has wavy blond hair and Raven's is jet-black. Definitely dyed. Oh, I get it now—*Raven*. Intermingled among the giggles and snickers, I hear: "freak," "burr butt," "weirdo," and "burr head." I ignore the names. It's easier that way. My eyes sweep the floor. Is it too late to sprint for the principal's office? But the students slow down as they reach my side, and their voices rise just enough that their words become clear.

"I heard her Dad was some kind of actor," says Madison, dressed in a designer labels, dramatically more chic than the majority of students.

After two seconds' hesitation, Donnie chimes in, "Yeah, some kind of faggoty actor."

I spin and face the group. Both boys, definitely tall enough to be basketball players, laugh heartily at Donnie's joke. The blond and miss dye job glare at me with contempt.

"What did you say about my Dad?"

Donnie hesitates, looks around at the group and grins menacingly in my direction. "I said he's an actor." Dramatic pause. "A faggoty actor." Donnie reaches up for a high five from Todd. Todd obliges and they smack palms in mid-air, above my head.

Too much! I drop my books, draw back my fist and swing widely toward the Donnie's face. First time I've ever tried to punch someone in anger. Second time I've thought about it this week. *What is happening to me?* My fist sails past his nose, missing him by several inches.

The group stares in amazement. Todd laughs piercingly then says, "Whooooah!"

"Hey psycho, I'm not gonna fight a girl," Donnie says as he takes one step back. I edge one step forward and swing my fist in a roundhouse motion toward his head again. This time I'm closer to the mark, but Donnie is faster. He drops his books, catches my fist with his right hand and swings us around.

The boy squares up and faces me, his back now to the trophy case. "I told you, Loony Tunes, boys don't fight girls in this town. I have no idea what things were like in whatever weirdo place you came from."

The group closes in and stares as seconds tick by. Waiting for my next move. Half a hallway past the office, the school janitor closes the door to his storage closet and wheels out his mop and bucket. The janitor, the tall, muscular African American man I saw in the hall the other day, limps noticeably as he pushes his bucket slowly in our direction.

Hollis walks out of the office and looks over at the scene to his side in front of the trophy case. He watches as I cock my fist back a third time. I glance toward the office as the door closes and see Hollis—watching. He stares directly at me and vigorously shakes his head no. Defeated. My shoulders slump, my head droops toward the linoleum floor. I drop my fist against my side.

Donnie glances at all of his friends in satisfaction and says, "Let's get out of here." As he straightens up from retrieving his books, Donnie stares in my direction with a cruel smile. He says, "Besides, I heard he's a dead, faggoty actor now."

White hot embers pierce my brain and instantly shoot into burning sparks behind my eyes. Lowering my head, I charge at Donnie with everything I've got. As the top of my head punches into his diaphragm, I feel, as well as hear, a distinct *woof* sound. Donnie doubles over onto my back and I churn forward with my legs. Grasping tightly behind Donnie's knees, I pull them into my chest. I lift the boy six inches off the ground and slam him forward with all my might. Churn my thighs for two steps until we hit something solid. A deafening explosion above, then on all sides of me.

I duck my head as glass rains down on Donnie and me for what seems like hours. The sounds of cracking and shrieking, while shockingly loud at first, eventually taper off and move further away. Footsteps race from the office and a man's hand yanks my back, with a vice-like grip, pulling me first up, then out of the trophy case. Under me, Donnie struggles for breath and only a gasping, sobbing sound escapes.

Down the hall, the janitor glances at the scene and shakes his head. He turns his mop and bucket around, heading back to his closet to exchange them for a push broom and dustpan. Just as he turns, his mouth twitches and pulls up into a grin. He limps down the hall and disappears into the closet.

CHAPTER SEVEN: THE TRIAL CAN PROCEED

Does anybody really want to think about a trip to the principal's office? Much less describe it? Not just any principal's office. One in a strange little town, where nobody knows me, but they all hate me just the same. I suppose the feeling's mutual. But I'm in this far, so I may as well keep rolling. You can just imagine the beginning; me sitting in the office outer room, the secretary's domain—stared at by every kid who comes through there. Even the sniffly middle schoolers whose parents send them to school sick, expecting the nurse to fix them up. Everyone thinking exactly the same two things. First, *I wonder what she did wrong?* And especially, *Thank God it's her and not me sitting there.* The longest minutes of a kid's life have to be the time spent waiting for her parents to show up at school when she's in trouble. Or in this case, the foster parents, or whoever Arvin and June are to me. Plenty of time to think about that one today.

The Spurlings showed up about an hour after the incident. Arvin looking sad and tired. June looking exasperated—bordering on downright angry. We didn't exchange a lot of pleasantries. The secretary whisked us into the big guy's office. No time to waste! We've got to deal with this juvenile delinquent. This threat to our community. This rabble rouser. The sooner the better.

I won't bore you with every little detail. You already know what happened. But I noticed that when they heard about the fight, both Arvin and June looked in amazement—first at me, then at the principal, then back and me and the principal again. Like watching a tennis match. I was embarrassed and scared as hell. But there's a tiny part of me, a part that I've never met before, that was just a little bit proud. Damn right I caused all this trouble. I sure did smash that trophy case to bits. And you better believe I kicked that jerk's ass. Oh Kayla, what are you becoming? What are we going to do with you?

Let's pick it up mid-sentence. These are

Principal Drake's words.

"…would normally be an expulsion, anywhere from three to five days. But I know there are extenuating circumstances in Kayla's situation, with what happened to her parents and all."

You know, the funny thing is I actually feel a little sorry for Mr. Drake. He seems like an alright guy. He's not having fun right now. He's just doing his job. That still doesn't make this any less excruciating.

Drake's not finished yet. "And we have the matter of the trophy case. While you were on your way, I called our supplier. He quoted me $400-$500 to fix the thing. Arvin, I know these are tough times, but you all are going to have to come up with that. The school board would ride me out of town if this comes out of our budget."

I glance over at Arvin, and he swallows hard. June looks at him, then at me—hard and angry. I can read her mind. This is not what she signed up for. No ma'am.

"But we can work something out, folks. I'm not going to ask you to come up with that kind of money all at once."

Arvin nods his head, stone-faced. That one hurts. But no way is he going to shirk his obligations. That's not the kind of man he is. That's not the kind of community this is. Back in Chicago, I've seen kids show up at meetings like this with a lawyer in tow. No kids are ever in the wrong there. No way would they cough up that kind of money without a fight. Things are different here. I did the crime. I'm glad I did it. I'd do it again. I'm hoping it doesn't come to that.

Drake is almost done. He's a busy guy. Things to do. People to see. "So we're going to compromise a little on Kayla's punishment. She needs to go ahead and serve one week of after-school detention. And Kayla…"

Here it comes. This is the hard part. He's been talking to the parents before. Now it's my turn.

"I don't care how much that boy provoked you or what he said. We don't handle things with violence around here. Or at least there will be consequences if you do. Do you understand me?"

I'm deep in thought. Nobody home.

"I said do you understand me, young lady?"

I nod and catch motion in my peripheral vision. Coming from the right. Wow, June is up and in my face—fast. "Kayla!"

"Yes. I mean yes, sir."

Not much to say about the car ride home. I start to explain what happened and June barks: "Quiet. We'll talk about it at home. Don't need to advertise our business for the whole town."

I didn't think the whole town could hear us in the car. But I'm down with that. Quiet works just fine for me. It's only a five minute drive from school to home, but it feels like an eternity. Einstein would have loved the way time slowed down in the car. Superman would feel like that car was a little Fortress of Solitude. If I were Superman, I could do that trick where he flew around the world really fast and made time go back a day. But if I were Superman, nobody would mess with me. But what if they didn't know that I was Superman? I think I understand how Clark Kent feels. Maybe I'm the Clark Kent of this town with powers that nobody knows about. Fat chance.

We're going to talk in the living room. Great. The living room that nobody uses except when company comes over. Maybe I'll be seen as company around here soon enough. June starts in: "Now listen here, girl. First of all, this is not the way we behave in this family. In this community. And what are you thinking? Fighting a boy? You could have gotten beat up, real bad."

"I'm not scared of him."

"He's not the one you need to be scared of right now!" June barks. Damn she's mad. Better take a different tack.

"He said things," I explain. "Bad things."

Arvin's turn now. "Kayla, people are going to say things to you your whole life. You can't go around fighting everybody who says something stupid."

"It was more than stupid. He was talking about my Dad. Called him names."

June, a little softer. "Well, that's not right. Not right at all. But you still can't go around fighting people. It's not ladylike and …"

"I don't care about being a lady." My turn to get mad.

"Well, you better start caring. You're growing up and no boy wants to be around a girl who gets in fights. It's just not civilized. It's not what proper Christians do."

Bite my tongue, hard. I'm not going there. At least not now.

"And, Kayla, you can't expect Arvin and me to come up with that kind of money to fix up that case. That's grocery money. No...we can't do it."

Try to regulate my breathing, slow down my heart rate. Untangle the knot in my stomach. I stare at my shoes. The little flower Geneva drew on my shoe is starting to fade. I'll have her draw something else.

"You're gonna need to get a job. After school, weekends, whatever and ..." The phone rings. June breaks off mid-sentence and heads for the kitchen, where the beige wall phone with the cord hanging down to the floor rests. I listen to June's side of the conversation. Just like I've seen Denise do several times. Hiding around the corner. When she thinks nobody is watching her. June comes back in. I can't believe that the cord stretches all the way from the kitchen to the living room.

"Arvin, it's for you. Emerson is on the

line."

He takes the phone from her and unwinds the cord, all the way back to the kitchen. I stand up to leave.

"Where do you think you're going? We aren't done here. Not by a ways. Stay right there while I start some water for supper."

Arvin talks. June cooks. And I sit. Alone is not bad. I might start calling this house my own little solitary confinement. I feel alone most of the time. Even when there are people around. Nobody likes me. And nobody wants me here. Except the little sweetie and she loves everybody and every living thing. She even likes those drooling, vicious mutts outside. I hear Arvin say "goodbye" and he talks to June. They whisper back and forth some and then come back. I can feel the tension begin to drift out of the air—just a touch.

Arvin's voice is hopeful. "Somebody up there is looking out for you, Kayla. That was Emerson...Mr. Pettus."

I must look confused, because Arvin explains: "He's the janitor over at the school. He saw what happened with the boy and talked to

Principal Drake. You're still in trouble and we've still got to make good on that case, but Emer...Mr. Pettus has an idea. He needs some help working at the school. Mornings. You could work mornings with him...before school. Mr. Drake said you can work from six-thirty to eight, mornings...every school day...for a month. That will cover the trophy case."

"Does she still get detention?" June asks.

"Yep. This is just to take care of the money thing. She still has to serve her time. Well, girl, what do you think?"

I start to nod and catch myself immediately. I guess you can teach an old dog new tricks. "Yes, sir."

"Well, good. You start tomorrow morning at 6:30 sharp. He'll let you in the back door. By the boiler room."

June breaks the tension ever so slightly. "Alright then, girl. Go on up and get on your homework. We'll have supper late tonight." She glances up at the clock "5:30. And get your own self up tomorrow. Don't even think about being late."

"No, Ma'am. May I be excused?"

"Go on, then."

I stroll out of the room and hit the stairs. Two at a time, turn the corner and head to my lair. Up the stairs and pull the cord up behind me. Flop on my bed and hug my oldest friend, Bun-Bun. He's always there for me. I really get how Dorothy felt when she said: *"People come and go so quickly here."* First that Donnie idiot, then Mr. Drake and now this Mr. Pettus. Oh Bun-Bun, I don't think we're in Chi-town anymore. Bun-Bun agrees.

CHAPTER EIGHT: MOCK TURTLE AND GRYPHON

It's not so bad getting up at 6 a.m. It's quiet. Peaceful. Arvin is already out the door, so I have the kitchen to myself. No Junior trying to slip pepper into my cereal. No Denise staring daggers at me (for no reason, I might add). I do miss hearing Geneva laughing over the comics. And then laughing again after I read them to her. No, this morning it's just me and my toast. From Gray's Bakery, where June works. That's all I need.

As I shove open the back door, there is Arvin's note—"Don't forget to feed the dogs. And June says to pick up some soup at the market after school." Crap, I don't have time for this. I can't be late for my first day of punishment—I mean rehabilitation, or restitution. Whatever. I use my shortcut system today. Lure the dogs into their houses with a biscuit, jump on the adjoining roofs and latch their doors behind them—fast! Then I get their bowls filled up with their foul smelling food from the feed store. Push the bowls in front of the doors and unlock the door with the rake. Just out of biting distance. When they bolt out of the doors, both dogs knock their bowls over—spilling their food onto the bare dirt. Not my problem. They'll eat it anyway.

Pull my bike from under the shed and I'm off. At the end of the driveway, I remember detention. I could do homework, but I'd rather read. Besides, I usually get my homework done in study hall. I'm one of the few kids who actually studies in study hall. I drop the bike in the yard and sprint into the house and up to my room. Push Bun-Bun aside and grab *Alice's Adventures*. Can't make it a day without my *Alice*. I run back out to my bike. Maybe track is my gig? Pedal out the drive and straight to school. No time for the grand Tour de Felton today.

I push open the back door to the school and head for the janitor's closet. Mr. Pettus is in there working, with the water running—his back to me.

"Hello…Sir?" Louder this time. "I'm here now."

Mr. Pettus jumps about two inches. "Girl, you almost gave me a heart attack. I unlocked the back door and then forgot that you were coming today. Must be getting old."

He doesn't look that old to me, but I keep quiet. Mr. Pettus adds some liquid soap to the water and pulls down two mops. He hands one to me and sets the other gently into the bucket. Doesn't spill a drop.

"So, you ready to get started?"

I nod and then remember myself. "Yes, sir."

"You don't have to call me 'sir.' I left the Corp eight years ago. I don't think we've properly met. I'm Emerson Pettus. But you better call me Mr. Pettus around here. Being school and all."

"Hi, Mr.... Pettus," I stutter. Not sure why I'm nervous. He seems nice. "I'm Kayla...Kayla Burbadge." I put out my hand and give him the grown-up grip that my Dad taught me.

"Wow, Kayla, you got some handshake. Are you a weightlifter?"

I chuckle. "No, I just did some work over the summer."

"I know you did. I was in that barn with you

and the men. Had my head all covered and a mask on. Keep out those nasty smells." He pauses and looks around. Rolls out a bucket he must have filled before I came in. "Anyway, let's get to work. Need to mop the gym and the cafetorium. Before the students start walking on it. Why don't you take the gym? You don't want to start with the junk you find on the lunchroom floor."

He grabs the bucket without wheels and leaves me the other. After a couple of steps, he's limping, unsteady.

"Mr. Pettus? Why don't we switch buckets? I can take that one."

He glances at his bucket then back at me. Just the hint of a smile. "OK, but it's heavy."

I grab his bucket and heave. Dang, he wasn't kidding. But I'm not backing down now. I take uneven steps toward the gym. Only spilling a little water as I go. I glance back and Pettus stares after me, shaking his head ever so slightly. A few more steps and I'm in the gym. Prisoner Burbadge, reporting for duty, as assigned. I dip the mop and start swabbing the deck. Just like Popeye. Wish I could punch like him.

School happens. No fights. No gum. No more trouble. Just lunch in the stands with Kenna Faye. Not bad for a Tuesday.

After school, I have another appointment—my first day in detention. The detention room is at the opposite end of the school from my locker. Normally, I'd hide out and wait for people to clear the halls. But I'm supposed to be there in five minutes. So I trudge through the unwashed masses (literally unwashed, I might add) and shuffle down the C hall to the detention room—what a study hall does in its spare time. There are half a dozen kids in the room already, scattered about. *They* are here. Sitting in the front nearest the door are the two boys I saw in the pool hall, cutting school the other day. The bigger one has kinky blond hair. Looks like he cut it himself. He's wearing a stained white tee—stained with either blood or ketchup. I don't want to guess. He's got a snake tattoo that starts somewhere on his chest and ends up with the fangs right at his jawline. Nice. The other one has dirty blond hair. I mean literally dirty. Like not washed in days. He is skinny and taller than his friend. Looks like he hasn't shaved in three days. He stares at me with those vacant eyes. Like nobody home. I stare back.

I start to take a seat one row over from them and immediately hear: "Kayla…Kayla Burbadge?" Another one who seems to know me. Am I wearing a name tag that I forgot? The detention monitor continues, "Please take a seat in front of me." She points to a chair on the opposite side of the room from the boys. Not in detention five minutes and I'm already in trouble. Where do they send kids who get in trouble in detention? Double secret detention? I snort and the teacher looks up at me, annoyed. Pull out my book and start reading. Wish I had a rabbit hole to fall into. Anything to get away from this place. I could stand a little Wonderland about now.

A half hour into detention, Mr. Pettus walks in and speaks privately to the teacher. I give a little wave, but he ignores me. "Mr. Sperry? Mr. Dole?" she asks. The boys snicker and mimic her saying 'Mr'. "Please accompany Mr. Pettus." The boys just sit there staring at the teacher, unblinking.

"Dave…Jimmy!" Mr. Pettus barks, getting their attention pronto. "Did you hear the lady? Get your butts up and move it. Now!" The boys shoot out of their chairs as if they were electrified. They look anything but defiant as they follow Mr. Pettus out the door and into the hall. The door slams behind them. I try to make out what is going on. Mr. Pettus does most of the talking. OK, all of the talking. Sounds pretty mad. I wonder what they did? That's too scary to think about, so I go back to my book. After about ten minutes, the boys return and immediately begin fooling around.

The bigger boy whispers "Did you get the same thing?"

His tall friend nods his head. "Yep. Says it's the last chance to stay on the team."

"Crap, you know that's a condition of..."

"Boys?" the monitor says. Do you want to spend the rest of the period with the principal?" They look down and shake their heads. Then both boys put their heads down on their desks and sleep.

At 4:15, the teacher stands and says. "Alright." The kids all jump up and I follow suit. The teacher quietly says: "Wait behind a minute." Great, now what did I do? It's always something around here. After the rest of the detainees leave, the teacher walks to the door and closes it. Here it comes. I'm heading to see the principal again.

"Kayla, I just want to warn you about those boys." I point to their empty seats and she nods. "You're new here, so you need to know. Stay as far away from those boys as you can. They are trouble waiting to happen. Do you understand me?"

I don't really, but I want to leave. "Yes, ma'am. Can I go now?"

"Yes, you *may* go," she corrects. Another grammar cop. I start toward the door, and she follows me.

"Just a minute, Kayla. Let me walk you out. I want to be sure they've gone." She grabs her sweater and bulky bag and strolls toward the door.

"Is someone picking you up?"

"No, ma'am. I rode my bike."

She smiles, almost friendly. "You don't need to call me ma'am. We never say ma'am or sir in Wisconsin, where I'm from. It makes me feel kind of old."

"Sorry. We didn't say it where I'm from either."

"We Northerners need to stick together."

She's being almost nice to me. Not what I expected from detention lady. I push open the creaking back door and unlock my bike from the lamp post. She waits till I push off and waves to me from the doorway. I wave back and my bike wobbles for a few feet.

    I need to ride through town on the way home. I'm supposed to pick up some Campbell's Soup from Haag's mini-mart. Haag's is kind of like a gas station store minus the gas. I heard it stays open pretty much on beer sales. People usually go to Sheffield for groceries. I pedal west on Washington Street, past Black Rock Hardwoods. I glance over, but the lights are all out now. Guess she closed up early. Turn left on Columbia and pull my bike in front of Haag's. No need to lock up. There's nobody else around. Like a Wild West ghost town. Only this is early 21st century and the Midwest.

    I wander around the store and check things out. Yep, the usual gas station stuff—pork rinds in eight flavors, mini hot dogs in a can, Snoballs, Twinkies and Hohos. All the good stuff. I snag an Almond Joy and head to the counter.

"Hey there, Kayla." How do they all know me? "Will that be it today, sweetie?" I pull out 75 cents and nod my head. "Say 'hey' to June and them for me." I smile at the girl, not much older than me, and nod again.

As I get to my bike, I remember the soup. Dang it. Maybe I'm the one getting old. I push the door back open and head for the soup aisle. Pick up a couple of cans of chicken noodle. Everybody's favorite. Mmm, mmm good, that's what Campbells soup is…I can hear them talking in the back room. They don't know I'm here.

"…you know...the one from Chicago. With the famous parents. C'mon, you know. That actor and the…the writer Mom. At least I think she was a writer. It's so sad. Killed by that semi-truck and leaving that poor girl an orphan. Heard the Mom was texting when she…"

I drop the soup cans and they roll down the aisle. Run out of the store, grab my bike and ride. Tears stinging my eyes. Hair whips my face. Can't see too well. Can't keep the bike straight. I'm gonna be sick. I stop my bike on a side street, beside a dark house and throw up next to some bushes. Scrape some leaves over the mess. Wipe my mouth, pick up my bike again and stand for a minute. I'm shaking too hard to ride, so I walk it toward home, two blocks away. Not my home though. My home is gone. Everybody in this town is talking about me…us. No wonder they all know my name.

CHAPTER NINE: THE CHESHIRE CAT SPEAKS

When Dad took me to Cubs' games five or six times a season, we always rode our bikes to the ballpark. If you live on the Northside of Chicago, it's really the best way to get to the game. Anybody who would drive is either a suburbanite or has insanely too much money. Who would pay $40 to have their car wedged into a lot where you probably can't get out for two hours? The buses and the El are fine, if you don't mind being jammed like a sardine next to a bunch of guys who reek of beer at noon. We could walk, but it's just a little too far. So biking down to the ball park was an awesome way to travel.

We always made it a point to ride down Alta Vista Terrace when we got near Wrigley. The street is one of the coolest streets in Chicago. It's built like a mirror. I know that doesn't make sense, but here it is. The first house on the Northwest corner of the street is exactly the same as the first house on the Southeast corner. Same with the next two and so on until you get to the middle and then each house is identical to the one across the street from it. Pretty crazy, huh? I recommend you check it out if you ever get to Chicago. Right now, I feel like I may never get back there.

Dad always wore sunglasses and his beat up old Cubs' hat. Wore the sunglasses rain or shine because he didn't want to have too many people recognize him. He always said that he loved his fans. But game days were special. That was his private time with his favorite girl. That's me. Was me.

I'm always amazed how just wearing sunglasses and a hat (and no makeup or wig, he reminds me) can make a person unrecognizable. When we pull into the fire station to park our bikes, the guys on the bench just wave. They've known Dad since before he was *the* John Burbadge. To them, he was just another Northside guy introducing his kid to the joy and heartbreak that being a Cubs fan is all about. Nobody special. Just one of the guys from the old neighborhood. Same way with the ushers and beer vendors and long-time season ticket holders who sat around us. To them he was the same little Johnny whose dad dragged him to the park thirty years ago. A tradition passed down for generations from father to son. And sometimes daughters.

I've been thinking about Dad's fame since I came to Felton. Now I understand it a little better. The whole town knows my story—like somebody took out a billboard. But they don't know me. They have no idea. The grownups seem to feel sorry for me, and the kids at school mostly ignore me. Or hate me. I'm a weird curiosity here at best. At worst, I'm…can't think about it anymore.

I've been working with Mr. Pettus before school for a little more than two weeks now. My time in detention is served and I'm more than halfway through my work detail. I don't mind it so much. It's quiet when I get up. And the fall mornings are really pretty now. I'm happy when I ride in the morning. Like I used to be. The rising sun lights up the stubble on the golden cornfields like an impressionist painting. I spent quite a bit of time in those galleries at the Art Institute in

Chicago. People come from all over the world to see Monet's haystack paintings. Now I get to see the real things. Something to think about.

For enforced labor, the work is not too bad. There is some heavy lifting, but I like being physically active. I also get to work by myself—the only time I can be alone in these hallowed halls. And Mr. Pettus is nice. He treats me like I'm…almost like an adult. OK, not really. But he treats me with respect. Not like some dumb kid. He asks me real questions about real things. Not like the teachers.

I'm running late getting my bucket back to the janitor's closet and the first kids begin to spill into the halls. Just a couple at first, then a wave. I pick up the heavy bucket and hustle around the corner to the custodian's room. Careful not spill any water. Because if I do, it's my job to mop it. Mr. Pettus says, "I ain't cleaning up after you and all these kids too." He's firm but fair.

As I near the closet, a bevy of girls seems to float around the corner. Wearing their skin-tight cheerleading outfits, my old friends Madison and Raven lead the pack, with an entourage trailing behind. Some are in cheer uniforms and some wear Felton spirit wear. "We've got spirit, how 'bout you?" they chant over and over with varying degrees of student response. Oh yeah, I got Felton team spirit running out my ears.

After Madison and Raven pass, I hear muffled comments and bursts of laughter which echo back through the ranks of their hanger-ons. I don't respond. I don't look up. I won't give the skanks the satisfaction. I'll deal with them in my own way. What my own way is, I have no idea. Following the girls, like hounds on the scent of a raccoon, are Donnie and Todd. I've learned about hounds, raccoons and other hunting stuff from Arvin. If a girl keeps her ears open around here, no telling what she might learn.

Donnie makes it a point to step right in my path—forcing me to stop on a dime. The dirty water sloshes to the edge of my bucket, but does not clear the rim. I hold the bucket at my side and pant—glaring up at the smirking boy.

Donnie snorts, "Hey Todd, guess they hire pretty much anybody to clean up the slop around here."

"Looks like you missed a spot over here," Todd drones, spitting his gum on the floor about six inches from my feet.

I see motion behind the boys and Mr. Pettus pushes through them, opening a hole like I've seen a Bears' blocker do for Matt Forte. He's my favorite player on my favorite team. Da Bears. Mr. Pettus strides unsteadily past the boys to my side where he spots the gum on the floor. Taking a paper towel from his pocket, he stoops down with a pained expression and scoops up the gum. Righting himself with surprising ease, he holds the gum out toward Todd. Todd stares at him with his usual expression—a sort of stunned stupor.

"Mr. Lazby, I believe this is yours."

Todd stares first at Mr. Pettus then over to Donnie, then back at Mr. Pettus. Donnie looks away and says nothing, taking just the slightest step back from Todd.

"Mr. Lazby?" Mr. Pettus asks, holding the gum extended toward Todd.

"Yeah, I was just getting ready to pick that up. It kinda fell out of my mouth," Todd says, his face turning pink and then crimson. Mr. Pettus stuffs the gum in Todd's hand and stands ramrod straight by my side.

"Mr. Barker and Mr. Lazby, do you have any business here?"

Donnie and Todd mumble something and shuffle to the side.

"I didn't hear you!" Mr. Pettus growls, scaring all three of us.

"No …um…no. We're just passing by on the way to class," Donnie says, quietly and insolently.

"Then perhaps you should carry on." Mr. Pettus extends his hand outward in a grand theatrical gesture. The boys walk away. As they get half a hall away, Donnie begins to imitate Mr. Pettus' limp. I suck in my breath and start to speak.

"Is he mocking my gait?" Mr. Pettus asks.

I stare at him in confusion.

"How I walk…my limp?"

I consider my response and then think back to Mom and Dad. They were big believers in that honesty thing. "Yes, sir," I respond quietly.

"Don't let those fools get under your skin. They're afraid of you because you didn't back down like everybody else. Stood your ground. Now they'll try whatever they can to get back at you. Just ignore them—that whole lot."

I shake my head and walk to the closet. Pick up my bucket—dang it's heavy—and pour the dirty water down the drain. Leave the bucket in the sink to soak. Eight minutes till the bell.

"Mr. Pettus, what happened to your…your leg?"

Mr. Pettus looks up at me with a shocked expression. My face flushes bright red, beaming hot. My cheeks are tingling.

"Oh…I...I'm so sorry. I didn't mean…"

"No, it's OK, Kayla. I'm just surprised because almost nobody ever asks about that. Thinks it will hurt my feelings or something. Not sure why. I know I don't have anything below the right knee. No national secret."

He looks at me and his expression softens. "The short version, 'cause you got to get to class. I was deployed in Iraq—Marine Corps. We were on foot patrol in a town called Fallujah. The area had already been cleared by the bomb squad, but I guess they missed one. I tripped it and everything went black—fast. When I came to in the hospital, they told me that a fellow Marine picked me up—185 pounds of me—and carried me on her shoulders two blocks to a safe zone. How she carried me, and how she didn't take fire, I'll never know. Guess God had other plans for me. Anyway, when I woke up, my toes were itching and I reached down to scratch them. They didn't know I was awake and nobody told me about the…uh, loss. Kind of a shock." He chuckles softly, then laughs at himself. "Yeah, I guess you could say it was a shock. I've had a few years to get used to it now." He glances down and taps his prosthetic foot on the floor—like he's tap dancing.

I stare at him in disbelief and he moves out of the doorway. "You better get to class. Don't want to be late and have to work here the whole semester."

"Bye Mr. Pettus and …" He looks at me expectantly. "I'll see you tomorrow."

"Bright and early girl. Bright…and…early."

I grab my backpack and head down the B hall to the music room. The beginning of another day! Let's sing!!

CHAPTER TEN: CURIOUSER AND CURIOUSER

One of the things I miss here is having friends. My old friends. From Chicago. It's like I fell off the face of the earth. No smart phone because we can't afford the old plan. No computer in the house. That's right, I do my homework during study hall or after school in the tiny computer lab (more like a computer closet). The computers in the lab block all social networking sites, so I can't check Facebook or anything from there. They probably cancelled my account anyway. None of my friends tried to track me down here. And who writes letters anymore? I know one person who does. June writes to someone in Indianapolis about once a week. Seems like a lot of effort to me.

If your friends don't stick with you when you're going through something bad -- something awful in my case -- are they really your friends? I sort of assumed that the guys and girls I knew from Northside Academy would be around forever. But I guess they've moved on. Scattered to their various high schools in Chicago—some public, some magnet school, some Catholic, a couple private schools. And here I am. Right here in bustling downtown Felton. I've only got one real friend—Kenna Faye. And she's been acting really weird lately. Staring off blankly into the distance. Looks like she's on the verge of crying. Won't say anything to me except mumbled responses. Just walks away without saying goodbye after lunch. Very strange. Have I done something wrong? If so, I don't know what it is.

    I'm in the last few days of my janitor work. You'll think I'm crazy, but I'm going to miss it. I'm really starting to like the work itself. Like I'm getting stronger every day. Checked out my arms in the mirror last night. Believe it or not, I'm getting some definition. If my friends back home knew I was looking at my arms in the mirror, they'd laugh at me. Friends? What friends?

    Mr. Pettus is pretty cool. Easy to talk to for an adult. Never pressures me to talk, but always seems interested in what I have to say. He's really funny in a way I'm not familiar with. When I commented that he doesn't sound like the other people around here, he explained the reason.

"I'm from Carolina," he told me proudly one morning. "A small town called Shelby—outside of Charlotte."

When I told him that June worked in Sheffield, right up the road, he launched into a history lesson. All about a Revolutionary War battle—The Battle of Kings Mountain. Imagine that—a history lesson before school even started. I paid attention because it was interesting.

When he finished his story, I asked, "How do you know all this stuff?"

"I was a history major in college. That's right girl, don't look so surprised. I got my degree from Appalachian State University. Don't even try to say the name, 'cause you'll say it wrong and I'll have to keep correcting you. Everybody around here says 'Appalachian' wrong. But let me finish up here so you can get to class," Mr. Pettus says, glancing at his watch. I never noticed before that he has an old fashioned kind of watch. The kind on a chain in your pocket.

Mr. Pettus stands and stretches. The warning bell rings and he looks up. Shoves open the janitor's closet door and the hall is jammed with kids. I was so engrossed in the story I didn't hear them.

"Two more days," he says grinning.

"What do you mean?"

"Only two more days on your work detail, unless you're planning to bust up anything else around here." He glares at me then lets out a belly laugh. "Now get on to class. See you tomorrow morning. And Kayla?" I spin around. "Remember the men in the battle I told you about? It's OK to be afraid. But a hero is somebody who faces their fears. Looks those fears in the eyes and says: 'You don't control me.' Do you know what I mean?"

"Yeah, I mean yes sir. I think I do."

He waves goodbye and I walk a few feet, then stop. I've got English first and it's my one class I really like. But I have time. He waves a big paw in my direction and I bolt for class. Hold the door, Mr. Chenoweth!

CHAPTER ELEVEN: WHAT THE DORMOUSE SAID

I seem to have more time in the mornings now that I don't have to go in and work. So I like to just ride my bike around and think. Before school starts and I have to think about things I don't want to. Mr. Chenoweth was talking about genres yesterday, and I started thinking about how we have to put everything in a neat little box. *Alice's Adventures in Wonderland* is a children's book. And it's also a fantasy. I wonder what the authors think about people trying to fit their book into some nice little category. I know I wouldn't like it. Probably because I don't think you can put people in a category. And authors are just people.

I mean who says that only boys can be on the football team and only girls care about English? Who made up those stupid rules about how the world works? It doesn't seem fair. It stops people from… what? What would they do if a girl wanted to play football? Probably freak out. And I know how much they tease any boy who acts like he's interested in *A Midsummer's Night Dream* or *To Kill a Mockingbird.* So most of the boys keep quiet in class, even if they like what we're reading. It's too bad, like they are having a part of their lives stolen by some small town, small-minded pettiness. It makes me sick.

I still park my bike in the back of the school past the boiler room. I skid to a stop, peel off my lock and start winding it around the frame. Then I smell smoke. On the other side of the dumpsters, two boys crouch down—smoking a cigarette. I don't think they heard me ride up. I stand silently and wait. Just wait.

"Dude, we better lay off these things or the first week's gonna be a bitch."

"Shut up. And don't remind me. That hell's about to start up again."

"It's our last year, though."

"You wish. No way you're gonna graduate."

"We shoulda run from this dump last year, when we had a chance."

"I'm not doin' that again. Hell, juvie's bad enough. And we both turn eighteen next year. I ain't doin' that kind of time—no way."

"So we just got to just stick it out here. That what you're sayin? For like a year?"

"Hell, it's only nine months now. Graduate and we can do what we want."

"I ain't no damn slave. He can't make me do that stuff anymore."

"Yeah, he can, dude. Part of the probation deal, remember? Do what he says or go back to juvie. Besides, you're lyin' if you say you don't like it. Beatin' guys' asses and gettin' away with it?" The other boy laughs. What are they talking about?

"Right, I forgot about that. Just hate the damn runnin.' And being ordered around."

"Hell, dude. Gonna be some guy orderin' you around your whole life. What difference does it make? Gimme a drag." He takes a long puff on the cigarette and then flicks the butt of the side of the dumpster. Sparks fly overhead and they both laugh.

The still-lit cigarette hits the ground and rolls under the dumpster near some trash. The boys start to walk around the bin and I move to the other side, as quietly as I can. They pull open the staff door and walk in like they own the place. How can they get in there? I catch a quick glimpse. The boys from detention! Something Dole…and what's the other one's last name? Perry? No, Sperry. When the door slams shut behind them, I find a bent stick on the ground. Stoop under the dumpster and stretch as far as I can. Snag the cigarette and roll it out to me. Unfiltered. Man, that stinks. Grind it out under my heel. I don't think those guys want to get caught burning down the school. At least unless they intended to. Off to math. I've got to get some help with that. Now that my mornings are freed up.

Lunchtime and I head to my usual spot. The bleachers loom ahead, but I know I'm nearing decision time. Already the fall days are starting to feel frosty in the morning when I ride to school. As I cross the baseball diamond and peek up, Kenna Faye is in her usual spot near the top. When she sees me walk up, Kenna Faye pulls herself slowly to her feet and makes her way awkwardly down the bleacher stairs.

"Hi KF," I offer hesitantly. She waves, but

shows no interest. "Kenna Faye did I..."

"No," she barks, cutting me off. "Nothing, just...nothing."

I watch her walk jerkily across the baseball diamond and to the school door. Hollis walks out and holds the door open for her. Kenna Faye enters without a word. Hollis looks after her and shakes his head.

"Hollis!" I shout from across the field. He looks up, smiles and walks over to me. Quickly, for a big guy.

I ask, "Do you know what's going on with Kenna Faye? Did I do something?" His smile drops quickly.

"Yeah, I've heard," he says. "Most everybody around here has."

"Well, I haven't heard."

He sighs and shakes his head. "Sherriff has been out to their trailer a few times. Kenna's mom has a boyfriend. A bad guy. He sells drugs ...and does other stuff."

"What kind of stuff?"

Hollis looks around nervously. "I don't want to say."

"Hollis, tell me!" I yell. A little too loud. He looks startled and turns red. "Sorry. Didn't mean to shout. But what's going on?"

"That guy has… I don't know how to…OK, I heard that when Kenna Faye's mom is gone, the guy pays attention to her. Not in a good way."

"Are you saying what I think you're…?" He nods, sadly. My face feels hot and my heart pounds. I've got a knot in my stomach again. I turn and walk toward school without looking back. This place makes me sick.

CHAPTER TWELVE: I'M BEGINNING TO GET VERY TIRED

For the first time in ages, I'm dragging getting out of bed. It's still dark. Cold and drafty up here. I…need…to …sleep… more. I think just ten more minutes will do it. *I'm moving to a place. It feels familiar, but I've never been there before. A man up ahead in old fashioned clothes motions for me to follow him. I feel like I should know him, but I can't see his face. Where is his face? He points up ahead. But I can't see anything. Not clearly anyway, just indistinct shapes moving quickly. Some move up, others down. Some stand up, some go to the ground. Moving, always moving. I ask the man "Sir, what does it mean?" I sense that he's smiling but I still can't make out his face. He turns and walks away—vanishing quickly. I start in his direction and...*

"Kayla Burbadge! I'm not calling your name

again. Get down here right now or you can deal with the truant officer yourself!" June screeches, clearly exasperated.

I tumble out of bed, grab the first pair of jeans and sweatshirt my hand hits (my unofficial school uniform) and run a hand through my stringy hair. Gross! My friends in Chicago would drag me to a salon if they saw me now. But the only salon in town is Marion's Stylette. I've seen the "before" and "after" pictures in their window. No thanks.

Push down my stairs, hustle down and the door slams up behind me. Uh oh. I've been warned twice about that before. Bounce down the main stairs and six sets of little eyes shoot my way. Two happy to see me and four not so much. Waiting until her mom turns her back, Denise sticks out her tongue at me. I give her a fake smile back and she scowls.

Geneva chirps, "Good morning, Kayla!" I pat her little back and she grins. Her face is covered with jelly and somehow a smudge of peanut butter has found its way into her hair. I grab a napkin and attack the hair problem first. The face will need a damp cloth after she's done.

Junior pretends to be engrossed in the comics from the morning paper. When June steps out the back door, he snaps a rubber band that pops me in the cheek, just below my eye.

"You little dirt bag," I hiss. "I'm gonna…"

"Mom, Kayla called Junior a 'dirt bag.' For no reason." Denise glances toward June with her sweet innocent look. I'd like to slap that look off her face.

"I'm sure Junior found some way to pester her. Now get on out of here and get yourselves ready for school." All bolt, but June grabs Geneva, and with one motion, twirls her up to her hip.

"Not so fast there, little lady. You need some work."

"Oh, Mommy, I'm fine."

"Yeah, you're fine all right. So sweet right now the ants will eat you on the way to pre-school. You don't want that, do you?"

Geneva looks up at her seriously, then over to me. "Will the ants eat me, Kayla?"

"No honey, your Mommy's teasing you."

June smirks, "Oh, was I now?" Then bends Geneva back and blows a raspberry on her stomach.

Geneva squeals with laughter. Clean face and all, she wriggles out of June's grasp and bolts out the kitchen archway. She stops on a dime, prances back in, giving me a big squeeze around the knees. I pat her head and look up at June, who shrugs and sets the damp beige dish towel on the counter.

You know how my school day went. Like they all do. Some reading, some writing, even a little algebra. But still no word on Kenna Faye. I haven't seen her around the last couple of days. Maybe she's out with the flu. Hope she's OK. Maybe I should call her. She might be mad at me though.

After school, I've got nothing going today. Arvin is taking Geneva for a checkup and the other two are playing at friends' houses. It still mystifies me that those two could have any friends. I guess there's somebody for everybody.

Got a couple of hours till it gets dark, I want to find a nice spot out away from here to finish re-reading *Alice in Wonderland.* For the fourth time this year. I was reading it when they…the accident.

I make my way to the back side of the school. Before rounding the corner I stop. No voices. Peer around the corner and it's empty. No Dole and Sperry. Those guys give me the creeps. Unlock my coil and wrap it around my seat post. Jump on and roll toward the parking lot. Something big moves into my peripheral vision. A red truck pulls up beside me as I ride, with a massive arm stuck out the driver's side window.

"Hey there, Kayla." Hollis grins shyly and points to the back of his battered pickup truck. "Do you want a ride home? I can throw your bike in the back."

"Hi Hollis." I keep pedaling, but as I veer away, he maintains speed with me.

"It's no trouble. I'm going your way anyway."

I brake to a stop and he pulls beside me. "What are you doing driving a truck? Are you old enough?"

"Yeah, I'm seventeen. Been drivin' for a year."

"But you're in my..." I stammer, not finishing.

"I got held back a year. Spent most of freshman year working with my Dad, after he took sick. And I still have some classes to catch up on. But I'm all legal and everything. I can show you my…"

"No, I believe you."

"Well, can I give you a lift?"

"I'm not…I'm going out for a ride today. Out in the country. I want to get out and see some things before it's too cold."

"But I can still take you," he pleads. "Wherever you want to go. I know all the woods around here. Been hunting them with my dad since I was a little guy."

I look up at him and smile. He gets it and starts to laugh. "OK, I was never a little guy, just smaller than I am now."

I shake my head. "No, I really want to just ride out and explore some alone. OK?"

"OK," he repeats, clearly disappointed. "But if you ever need a ride…anywhere…I can take you. Dad doesn't need the pickup as much once we get the crops in. It's our slow time."

"Thanks, Hollis. See you tomorrow."

"Bye Kayla. Ride safe," he says. "And watch out for those combines. They take up the whole road."

"I will," I say, waving goodbye and pushing off at the same time. I roll through town, ride past our street and head south onto County Road 800 East. Not sure where it will take me, but it looks pretty. Pedal for a couple of miles past acres and acres of corn stubble—dead corn stalks as far as the eye can see. It's a cold, sad looking place this time of year. Everything dead and brown. Wish I had a camera. This would make a cool art collage. I stop at the first intersection and think about where I want to go. River Road looks interesting. There is an old cemetery about one hundred feet from the intersection. But I ride a bit further on 800 East until I come to a bridge over a small stream.

I lay my bike down off the road, pick up some small sticks and start throwing them in the creek. A memory floods my mind and I run to the other side of the bridge. My stick appears and I cheer. I won! Pooh sticks! But I can't really win if there isn't somebody else to play. Should have brought Bun-Bun.

Just then a car approaches—heading right for the bridge and my bike. I jump up and wave my hands to signal stop! Can't see the thing from the glare of the sun. I squint at the driver.

"This is not the right place."

"Who is…Hollis, is that you?"

Hollis repeats, "This is not the right place."

"What place are you talking about? And why are you following me?"

"The place you're looking for. The one from your Dad's movie. The bear movie. This isn't the right place, but I can show you the…"

Slowly, I realize what he's talking about. *The Fire Bear* movie. Forgot that Dad actually picked some of the shooting locations from places he used to run around when he was a kid. Duh!

"I wasn't looking for that place. Or any place. I just wanted to ride my bike and be alone. OK?"

"OK," he repeats, obviously hurt. "I just didn't want you to get lost out here. I've lived here my whole life and I know…"

"Hollis, I'm fine. I know how to get back home." Right. Just like Dorothy. Just like Alice. Just like Meg from *A Wrinkle in Time*. I could use a little time warping right now.

"OK," he says sadly, turning his truck around barely missing a three foot drop off. "But if you ever want to see that place. You know, the Black Gulley. I can take you there. It's a real place. Those explosions were real…not made up."

I have no idea what he's talking about. But the afternoon is fading fast and I want to explore some more. "I'm fine, Hollis. Thanks for checking on me. But I'm fine. I'll see you in school tomorrow."

He waves goodbye and bangs three times on the side of his truck as he drives away. I sigh and drop my Pooh sticks. It's no fun playing alone. Pick up my bike and ride back up to the intersection. Turn left on the River Road and pedal over to the cemetery. A dirt road veers off to the left. Drop my bike outside the fence. No need to lock. Nobody's stealing it way out here. The cemetery gates look ancient. Iron and rusting—big time. Scrawled over the top of the main gate is the name: Van Wyck Cemetery. What is that? German, Dutch…something like that. I think Van means "from". So maybe they were from the town of Wyck. I'll look it up when I get home. How did those Europeans end up way out here? In the middle of nowhere. Come to think of it, how did I end up here? In the middle of nowhere.

There is no lock on the gate and no sign saying to stay out. I gently push the gate open and it creaks loudly. A flock of crows lifts off the ground cawing angrily. I've disturbed their hunt for dinner. Sorry guys. The graves at the front look new. A few from this year. One even has fresh dirt. No grass growing over Mrs. Thompkins yet. As I make my way to the back of the graveyard, I notice a difference. The gravestones are much smaller. Some are broken. Others are black with age. Some are covered with lichens, others with green mold. Clearly this cemetery started off way back here. A long, long time ago. It's not cold out but, I shiver—just a little. I'm not cold and not scared. I feel kind of…anxious about this place.

I think of a fun game. Find the earliest birth date. Here's a Wallace born in 1821—in Scotland! Here's a Van Pelt born in 1806—in North Carolina. Here's a Boyd born in 1798—can't make out the birthplace. I can't believe it. They've been dead and buried here for two-hundred years. My head starts spinning, thinking about all that time. I need to move. There's no fence in the back. The earliest graves sit just up a small bluff from a pretty little creek. I set down my backpack, pull out my spare jacket and lay it on the bluff, just above a small bend in the creek. I lie down on the jacket and take out my book. There is a ripple in the creek that sounds like the fountains I used to hear back at The Edgewater Garden Shop in Chicago. I like it here. It feels …what? Safe. Peaceful.

I close my eyes and think about Alice. She chose to go down that rabbit hole. When things got crazy, she adjusted. Made do. Figured out a plan to fit into her new world. But when things got too crazy, she said, "Adios. I'm outta here." I didn't choose to go down this rabbit hole. And I sure as heck have nowhere to go back to. So where's that leave me. Adjust? Change? Fit in? That's a great concept, but how? I don't have any idea and I…

The man appears again. This time across the creek. Dressed in old fashioned clothes. Like some frontier guy. He waves for me to cross the creek and join him. He seems friendly enough. Harmless. He's pointing up ahead and motions for me to join him. I've got nothing better to do. I was looking for an adventure today. I walk to the man's side and he points into the distance. Starts walking and I catch up with him. We walk together through a clearing, then into a densely wooded area. After five minutes of walking, we come to a steep ravine, cast in early evening shadows. The man points down into the ravine. I'm afraid to go. He reaches down and takes my hand. Suddenly I feel safe, strong, alive. When we get to the base of the ravine, I look up at the man. "Who are you?" I ask. The man looks down and smiles. All at once, his features become crystal clear and I gasp. "Daddy? How did you get here? What is...?" He looks up and there is movement at the far end of the ravine. A sort of glow. Getting brighter, bigger, closer. The indistinct shape seems to be constantly changing. At first I think it's a woman. Then it morphs into some kind of an animal. A big animal.

The man drops my hand and points toward the thing, moving slowly—closer to us by the minute. "Daddy, what is it?"

For the first time he speaks. It's my father's voice, but his words sound like music, rich and flowing. "You've got to go alone, Kayla. Face the bear alone. You can do it, honey. You've got everything you need inside you. Face the bear."

I look up to ask him what to do, but he's gone. Like he never existed. But the bear's still there. Getting brighter and clearer every step it takes toward me. I can feel the heat as it approaches. Slowly but surely. Step by step. When the bear gets within ten feet, I feel its intense heat, but it doesn't burn me. I remember my father's words and I stand straight and tall, facing the bear. I take two steps toward the creature, then it takes a couple of steps toward me. I've never been this close to a bear before and don't know how to act around it. I take the final three steps and the bear sits down, directly in front of me. Then it does the strangest thing. Ever so slowly and gently, the bear puts its massive head on my left shoulder and snuggles up against me. Its fur is warm and soft. The bear turns its snout toward my face and starts licking. Tentatively at first. Then more and more, faster and faster. It tickles and I giggle.

"There she is." A man's voice.

"Yeah, it's Kayla."

"Is she OK? Doesn't look hurt. Tige! Prince! Get off that girl," says Arvin.

I open my eyes and look up. Two big gross slobbery dog snouts are about three inches from my face. The black one takes one final lick on my tear-stained cheek, then runs off and sits by Arvin's side.

I glance around and see Mr. Pettus looking at me, all concerned. Hollis is there too and some man I've never seen before.

"Are you OK, Kayla?" Arvin asks, with genuine concern.

I notice for the first time that there's just a sliver of light left in the sky. All of the men are holding flashlights, which play eerily off the gravestones and trees swaying in the light breeze. I look across the creek. Nothing.

"I'm fine, but did you see that thing?"

"What thing?"

"That bear…the glowing bear? It was just across there down that hill where the man…"

"There's no bears around here, Kayla," Arvin says, smiling. "I've lived near here my whole life and never seen anything bigger than a deer. How 'bout you, Hollis?"

Hollis shakes his head no. He studies me like he's got a question to ask.

"C'mon, let's get you home, girl. You got June all worried sick. We'll throw your bike in Hollis' truck, and he can drop it by the house." Hollis nods and picks up my bike with one hand—like it weighs a few ounces.

I follow Arvin to the truck and the dogs walk placidly by his side, looking up to him for instruction. I have to ask: "Why aren't those dogs acting all mean and crazy like normal?"

"I told you, girl, they're nice dogs. They just don't take to being chained up is all. Knew you'd get to like them. Once you knew 'em." He points to the back of his truck and the dogs jump in, obediently. "Dogs don't like to be chained up," he says. Something to think about.

Back at the house, Hollis lifts my bike out with one hand and rolls it to me. He stares at me for a while. I can tell he's got something on his mind.

"Want to have lunch tomorrow?" he asks hesitantly.

"I eat with Kenna Faye and…"

"You haven't heard?"

"Heard what?"

"Her Mom found out what the boyfriend was doing and sent her away for a while. With some relative. Until she can get that guy out of there."

"How long will she be gone?" I ask, stunned.

"I don't know. A couple of weeks. Maybe more. But she'll be..." I don't hear the end of his sentence. I'm done with this place. I grab my bike and rip off the lock. Sling it hard over my back and the padlock knocks a welt to the right of my spine. Good. I like the pain. Slam my bike down outside the back door. Let the stupid thing rust in the rain. I don't want it anyway. The house is quiet. The others are in bed. I stomp up the stairs and pull down my attic trap door. Run up as fast as I can and pull the door hard up behind me. It slams so hard it hurts my ears for a few seconds. Climb into bed, pull Bun-Bun to me and cry. For Kenna Faye. Then for Mom and Dad. I miss them so much! Finally, for me. I cry for me because...because who else will do it? I cry till no more tears will come, then wracking sobs into my pillow. Harsh guttural sobs at first, then gentler, easing, quieter. Until I hear somebody snoring in my room. Then I don't. It's black outside. The rain has stopped, but the wind moans and shakes my window. Black.

CHAPTER THIRTEEN: DRINK ME

"Kayla, are you comin' down for breakfast?" It's June. Are they eating breakfast for dinner? "Kayla, time to get up for school."

"I'm not going to school." Is that my voice? Sounds like a scratchy old record. "I'm sick." It's true. I'm sick alright. Sick of how people treat other people. Sick of being here. Sick of being the weirdo misfit. Sick of being the outsider. I'm sick of my life.

"I'll let them know that you're comin' down with something. Can I bring you anything before I go to work? You want some juice? Or a piece of toast? Anything?" June is trying her best to be nice.

"No. I just want to sleep."

"Alright, girl. I'll see you when I get off this afternoon. Just call the bakery if you need anything, hear?"

I don't respond. Roll over and sleep again. Weird dreams. About places I've never been. Things that I don't understand. *A large room with squares laid out like a checkerboard. I'm way above the room looking down on it and there's a hive of activity on the squares. Lots of people in strange dress, moving constantly. Like a giant, complicated dance with no music. A dance I definitely don't know the steps to. The people move and move and move effortlessly. With strength and beauty. Suddenly a shrill whistle blows and the dancing stops. The dancers all turn and look up at me. Like they are expecting something. They want something from me. What do you all want? I don't....*

Wake again and it's dark. No, just the tiniest sliver of twilight glowing in the western sky. The rain has stopped and the wind is calm. The storm has passed. My clock says 5:52. Is that A.M. What day is it? I catch a whiff of my clothes. Gross! Sneak a peak in the mirror and a witch stares back at me. All gnarly hair and deeply lined, tear-streaked face. I'm sleeping beauty alright. I'm sure the princes are just lining up down there on Porter Street to rescue me from my tower. Push open the staircase and stumble down toward the hall bathroom.

At the top of the stairs, I hear voices. Adult voices. Are they having a party down there? I listen closer and recognize a couple. There's the principal. June and Arvin. And one more. It's Mr. Pettus. I keep hearing one thing over and over. Kayla this…Kayla that. They're talking about me. Can't wait to hear what they've figured out about the wacko witch upstairs. The crazy girl in the attic. Me.

Decide that a shower's in order. Miraculously, it's free. I turn the shower up as hot as I can stand it, then a few degrees hotter. I need to burn these feeling out of me. Got to get back to…I would say normal, but there is no normal here. Got to get myself to someplace else. Something else. I want to be somebody else. After my shower, it's back to sleep again.

Found out what the little grownup party was all about last night. Surprise! It was about me! Turns out that they're all worried just because I missed a day of school. And cried a little. What's the big deal? Guess I'm freaking everybody out with all my crying, acting out and now skipping school. I've become a regular delinquent since moving here. But they all agreed that *something must be done.* They all want to fix me. Good luck with that. Meanwhile, my old buddy Mr. Pettus found out about how goofy I've been acting (bad news travels fast around here). He got all worried about me and came up with a plan. Pitched his plan to all of the conspirators and everybody gave it a thumbs up. So I'm the subject of a plan. A plan to fix me. I'm all ears.

So here's the plan. Here's why I'm up dressed with my jacket on at 6:00 am on a Saturday before the damn sun is even up. Mr. Pettus and Hollis and I are going on an outing. A fishin' trip. Oh joy. So Mr. Pettus honks the horn, I grab my toast, quietly close the front door and head for his pickup. Is it just me or does every person in this town drive a pickup? There's another pickup parked behind Mr. Pettus, and I see Hollis' shaggy head sticking out the window. He bellows out, a bit too enthusiastically, "Mornin', Kayla!" I give him a wave and a tiny smile. Pull open the creaky passenger door and slide into the seat of Mr. Pettus' car. He has the heat cranked up and the seat feels warm.

"How you feelin' this morning, girl?" Mr. P asks. "You ready to catch some fish?" I shrug and look up at the horizon—the sun just beginning to peak up all gold over the distant cornfields. The extent of my fishing experience was to stay up all night once a couple of years ago smelt netting with my Dad and his buddies on Lake Michigan. You only fish for smelt at night. Catch these little sardine-looking things and fry them up and eat them right there on the shoreline. Not sure that it's really fishing. More of an excuse for an all-night beer drinking party for the men. But I was happy that Daddy thought I was grown up enough to tag along with the guys. I'm guessing this fishing will be a little bit different.

Mr. Pettus makes small talk along the way. Nothing serious. No probing questions. I like that. Mostly, we listen to Motown music and look out the window as the fields go by. In twenty minutes, he enters a tight turn, honks his horn and then creeps around the corner. Under an ancient railroad bridge. Just past the bridge, a small creek meanders under the road. We pull to the side of the road, just past the creek.

Fishing out here is actually kind of fun. I catch my first bluegill, then two crappies. I'm starting to get the hang of this. I even learn how to take the hook out of the fish's mouth without getting stung by its spiny things. After a couple of hours, Mr. Pettus sends Hollis back up to the truck for lunch.

He says, "Hollis, would you give Kayla and me a few minutes to talk? In private?" Hollis nods and makes his way slowly to the car, whistling a song I heard a long time ago on the radio. Something about a train and New Orleans.

"Thanks for bringing me out here, Mr. Pettus," I say. "This has been fun. The fishing and the creek and everything."

"Glad you're here…and feeling better. Back to school on Monday?"

"Yes, sir. I'll be there."

"Good girl. Now there's one more thing I want to ask you. You don't have to answer me now. But I want you to think about it."

What's this about?

"At the school, I coach a team. A wrestling team. Well, we're not officially a school team. More like a club. But all of the guys on the team are students at Felton. Except my son, Emmy. He goes to school down in Columbus. Anyway, we got a couple of openings on the team. One for a lightweight wrestler. Under 106 pounds."

Wonder how he knows how much I weigh? And where is this going?

"So I was wondering if you'd like to join the team."

I laugh "Really?" He nods. "You're not joking?" I ask.

"I'm very serious. I've seen you handle some heavy weights. I can tell you're strong for your size. And you're not afraid of getting physical." He smiles knowingly.

"But I can't wrestle against boys…I don't know anything about wrestling and I…"

"I know a lot about wrestling. I wrestled in college. That's my job as the coach. To teach you. None of these boys knew anything about wrestling before I got here. And we've got a few pretty good guys now."

"But it would be really weird—a girl wrestling against boys. Is it even allowed?"

"Yes, it's allowed. There are a few girls wrestling on teams here and there. Not too many. But the number is growing. And some of them are pretty good. There was a girl here in Indiana made it to the state tourney last year.

"I don't know, Mr. Pettus. I don't think I could do it. I just…"

"Don't answer right now. Just promise me one thing."

"What's that?"

"Just think about it. And come out and see a practice someday next week. We work out from four to six o'clock at the old Meredith barn. You remember that place?"

Oh, yeah. I remember spending weeks cleaning cow crap and other disgusting stuff out of there last summer. I nod my head.

"So, think about this for a while. Let me know in a few days." A twig snaps behind us and Mr. Pettus turns toward the sound. "Hey, here's

Hollis with our fried chicken. Shall we give these fish a break for a while?"

I stare at the creek and think. Wrestling? Really? Wrestling? Now there's a rabbit hole that even Alice would run away from. I think I'm ready to start a new book.

CHAPTER FOURTEEN: THE WOOD IS WILD

Wednesday. Five-fifteen. I'm here, but I don't know why. It's a waste of time. Suddenly, the weather has turned nasty. It's cold, and the biting north wind whips through my thin sweats like driven rain through a screen door. Why did I wear these cheap things here? Why am I even here? I should be up in my little room reading my new book—*The Wind in the Willows*. I peer through the cracked opening of the creaky barn door into the dimly lit interior. The smell of sweaty boys assaults my nose as I catch glimpses of movement. First nothing, then fierce action and immediate response. I turn to leave and the wind shoves me roughly into the barn door.

As I rest and prepare my exit strategy, the door pushes against my back side. I force myself to the right and a giant figure strides through the opening and into the biting winter air. His dark blue sweatshirt appears nearly black with sweat in the late afternoon light. The boy wraps his arms around his massive upper body to shield himself against the November cold. Hollis squints into the pale final twinges of daylight and spots me, smiling with recognition.

"Kayla...great," Hollis says. "I didn't think you were coming."

"I'm not coming."

"But you're here. Did you check it out?"

"No...OK, I watched a little. So?"

"So, what do you think?"

"About what? The state of the economy?"

Hollis drops his arms to his sides and laughs. "What do you think about joining the team?"

"I don't really see myself as a joiner. You may not have noticed, but I'm a bit more of a do-it-yourself kind of girl."

"But the team needs you. We don't have anybody wrestling 106 pounds."

"How dare you guess at my weight." I scowl until Hollis' face drops—hurt. I allow myself a brief smile. "And what's this about 'we'? What are you doing in this sweaty mess?"

"I joined the team."

"Since when?"

"Since Monday. Coach talked to me down at the creek last weekend and explained the situation. We have every weight class filled except 106 and heavyweight."

"So, you're wrestling 106?" Hollis seems confused for a moment, then chuckles.

"You're quite a comedian today. You could take your act up to the comedy club in Indy. But seriously, come on inside and meet the guys."

"I'm not going to wrestle."

"Why not?"

"Duh, I'm a girl -- they're boys."

"There are lots of girls in wrestling."

"Really?"

"Well, not a lot—but a few. And some of them are pretty good. Did you hear about that girl who made it to the state finals last year?"

"I lived in Chicago last year. I was a little out of the Indiana wrestling loop."

"I know. But you could still help the team

out. We need you."

"Get somebody else."

"Besides, I saw what you did to Donnie that day. And he had about sixty pounds on you."

"I was mad at that asshole."

"Well, you shouldn't get angry on the mat. Coach says it works against you."

"Since when are you and Mr. Pettis so tight?"

"Coach's helped me a lot. He can help you too."

I spin and stare daggers at his face—a foot over my head. "I don't need anybody's help. I can help myself."

"Everybody needs help sometime." Hollis looks at me with—damn, is that pity?

"It will never work. Those guys would just laugh at me." I point through the barn door.

"Nobody laughs at anybody on the wrestling mat. Coach says one of the bravest things you can do in life is step on a wrestling mat—alone."

"Again with the Coach sayings. Has he written a book with all of his tidbits of wisdom?"

Hollis laughs again before turning to gaze

through the crack in the ancient door. "Break's almost over. What do you say? Would you at least give it a try?"

"Hollis, they don't need me. They'll do fine with all the other guys."

"There's something else I haven't told you. It's important. If we win just one dual meet this year, Principal Drake said he'll recommend that wrestling become an official school sport."

"OK. So what?"

"So, Coach Pettis needs that coaching job. And he gets hired as a P.E. teacher. He needs the money to move his family here. So they can be together again."

I sigh and hang my head. "I didn't know that."

"I'm not just doing this for me. Or even for the other guys. I'm doing it for Coach."

I stare up at Hollis blankly, then turn my face into the bitter wind again.

"So what do you say? Just try one practice. You'll learn a lot and the guys will help you. Some of them have been through some rough times, too."

"I don't know. I just…"

"Try it. Just one practice. Then make up your mind."

With my back to Hollis I roll my eyes. The wind drives tiny pellets of stinging wet into my cheeks. I blow out my breath and turn slowly. Hollis has opened the barn door and the smell of boy stink rolls out in waves. I make a face.

"I told Mr. Pettus I'll think about it. So, I'll think about it. But I'm not making any promises."

"Great!" Hollis beams. "I think you'll love it. You'll see." He peers into the barn. "I gotta go. See you later." He closes the barn door behind him, taking the reeking body heat inside the aging building. Where I spent so many lovely hours this summer. This summer. Seems like a lifetime ago.

"What am I gonna do about this?" I moan into the brittle darkening sky. The wind responds with a howl through the empty branches of the massive oak tree overhead. I yank my bike off the peeling paint on the barn and push a few feet before jumping on, the gravel crunching under my tires. Into the frigid Indiana night.

CHAPTER FIFTEEN: SOMETHING ABOVE, CALLING IMPERIOUSLY

Thursday morning. Riding my bike to school, the long way. Man, it's getting cold. I need to start wearing more layers. And gloves and hat would probably be smart. You'd think I've never lived in a cold climate before.

Decision, decisions. Before I moved to this place, I was a pretty decisive person. If my friends couldn't decide between Thai and Indian for lunch, I was usually the deciding vote. If the question was music and a burger at Kura's Corner or music and a veggie burger at the Heartlfelt Café, I could make the decision. Swimming at Montrose beach or rollerblading on the lakefront. Why not both?

But this wrestling thing has me stumped. On the one hand, the idea is ludicrous. I'd be humiliated on so many levels. If people thought I was freak before, what would this do to my reputation? And I can't imagine going out in front of all those people just to let some guy beat my brains in. It's crazy, right?

On the other hand, Mr. Pettus has been really nice to me, and I'd like to try to help him if I can. And what do I care about what the kids here think about me? Can it really be any worse? I've never backed away from a challenge. Once in Michigan, my friends dared me to stand in the woods alone, without a light, for 15 minutes. I stayed 20. They were freaked out when I came back. Thought I was eaten by a wild animal. But the most attractive part of this wrestling thing is to learn a new skill. I read a few articles Mr. Pettus gave me about girls who have wrestled. They all said that it was really hard, in a lot of ways. But they also said that it helped them grow and gain confidence in themselves. I could use some of that medicine.

So I'm thinking and thinking and thinking. To be or not to be (a wrestler)? I might be good at it. And I'm not afraid to wrestle a boy. Doesn't mean anything to me. But what if they laugh at me? Hollis says that nobody laughs at anybody on the wrestling mat. Hollis…he's a wrestling expert after three days of practice. It would be nice to be part of something…something bigger than just me. A team. I was on a couple of girls softball teams back in Chicago. But nobody was serious about it. Just some goofy girls fooling around. I think this wrestling thing would be different... really different.

Wish I could talk to Kenna Faye about it. Get her advice. But she's been gone for two weeks now. Not sure when she's coming back. If ever. I'm gonna need to make this decision on my own. Definitely can't talk to June and Arvin about this. They would think I'm nuts. What to do?

Dad always said that when life takes away one thing, you get something else in return. Lose one part in a movie and another one pops up. But this can't be the kind of thing he was talking about. I lost my whole family. And this is just a stupid wrestling team. Other than Hollis, I don't even know any of the guys on the team. Are they like the other jocks at this school? Obnoxious self-centered jerks like Donnie and Todd? Does the wrestling team have an entourage like Raven and Madison and their posse of hangers-on? Why did Pettus put me in this position? Aren't there any other little freshman boys that he can get for his team? Why me?

OK, I need to decide this once and for all. I need a sign. To my right, just up a driveway, two little boys play basketball on a hoop tacked up to the side of their garage. They are arguing over whose turn it is to shoot. One boy tries to keep the ball away, but the other knocks it out of his hands. The ball rolls away and down a small hill. The taller boy grabs the other and throws him to the ground. The boy on the ground grabs the pants leg of the other kid and they roll around in the grass. Over and over and over until one of the boys ends up on top. He puts his knees on the other boy's shoulder and says: "Say uncle." The kid on the bottom won't say it. Instead he pitches the boy off and jumps on top. They roll a few more times, then one boy jumps off the other and runs to retrieve the ball. Grabs it and throws it up the hill to his friend. When he gets back to the driveway, his friend throws the ball back and they continue their game. Is that my sign? Probably not.

I know men have been wrestling since the first Olympics back in Greece. Boys are always wrestling around—just for fun. But I don't know about girls.

Pull up to school and lock my bike in the usual place. The smokers are nowhere to be found. One final look at the sky before I start my day. Just then, the sun peeks out from behind the gray/black clouds and sprays a shaft of golden light on a lone bare tree in the middle of the cornfield next door. It's really pretty. Still not a sign.

I don't really need a sign. I'll decide on my own. OK, damn it. I'll do it. Talk to Mr. Pettus at lunch time today. At least I'll have someplace warm to sit in the janitor's closet.

Instead of heading to my usual spot in the bleachers, I make my way to an old familiar territory. One which very few students know exists, much less ever visit. My old haunt, the janitor's closet. Mr. Pettus is fiddling with the dial of his radio. It doesn't get good reception in here. And he's got very specific taste in music. "None of that awful top-40 garbage. Doesn't matter if it's Black or white top 40. It's all garbage." I've heard him say that more than once. Since I'm a visitor here now, I knock. He spins deftly on his artificial leg and looks up with a smile.

"Hey, Kayla. How you doin'?"

"I'm good. Mind if I join you for lunch. I won't eat much of yours. I promise." This was a joke we used to share. He'd ask if I wanted a bite of his breakfast. Then claim I ate the whole thing. I only had a couple of bites.

"Sure, pull up a throne and sit down." What he calls thrones are really old cable spools. Just the right size for a little chair—and stackable. He glances over from his sandwich. "What's up?"

"Not much. I've been thinking about what you asked me. And I stopped by the barn yesterday."

"Hollis told me you were there. You should have come in."

"I wasn't ready yet."

"And now?"

"I've decided." No need for dramatic buildup. Here goes. "I'll try it. But I don't think I can help you."

"You let me worry about that. And I'm happy you'll be part of the team. Can you start tonight?"

"I don't have any equipment. I don't even know what I need."

"For tonight, just bring your gym clothes. I'll figure out a place for you to change. Then you can meet the guys, go through warm-ups and just watch how a typical practice goes. You can learn a lot about wrestling by watching."

"But will I need a uniform?"

"I'll get you shoes and a headgear. We have team uniforms for our meets. For practice, you'll need some compression shorts. To wear under your gym shorts. And you also need…" He hesitates and looks me over.

"What?"

"OK, I haven't dealt with this before. But I think it would be a good idea if you got a sports bra. Do you know what that is?" Nod my head. Of course I know what that is. Just have to find one.

"So we'll see you at four at the barn. Hollis can give you a lift over if you like."

"No, I'll ride." I want to continue riding my bike until it's too cold.

"OK, great. See you then. And Kayla." I turn back to the closet as he stands to see me out.

"I'm really glad you'll be joining us. You made a good decision."

We'll see about that.

When I arrive at the barn after school, there is a lot of activity. Some guys are running around on the mats. Others are throwing a ball around, trying to hit a square taped up on a barn wall. One kid sits on the ground reading, ignoring the noise, totally absorbed in his book.

"Hey, Kayla!" Hollis sees me first. When he says my name it's like a power switch is thrown off. All activity and noise stops. Twelve boys freeze and stare in my direction. All except the kid reading his book. I stare back, like a deer trapped in the headlights of a car—a car about to run over it.

A whistle blows from the corner. Mr. Pettus strides in. He has a different prosthetic device on his leg. It's curved and smooth on the bottom. Like that runner in the Olympics. "What's the matter with you guys? Act like you've never seen a girl before." A ball bounces. "Mike, Jako, put the ball down. Practice has started." The ball rolls over into a corner, bounces off the wall and stops.

"OK, everybody listen up. This is Kayla

Burbadge. She'll be our new 106. Some of you guys probably know her from school." Hollis waves, but the other guys stand frozen. Still staring.

"Kayla. These guys will be your teammates. You'll get to know them well over the next four months. They'll be going into battle with you. Well, they'll be supporting you anyway. You go into battle alone." I swallow hard and stare back at the boys. No way am I showing them how damn scared I am.

"Let me introduce everybody. Our 113 pounder is Arthur Boxell. He'll be your workout partner." The boy with the book. He steps forward formally and shakes my hand. Makes eye contact for the first time. A good looking kid with dark skin and jet black, longish hair. Maybe Middle Eastern or Indian?

"Next is Stefano. Where's Mendez?" A short Latino guy raises his hand from the back row. "Couldn't see you behind those giant trees." The boy laughs.

"Our 126 is Bao Tran." He's either Thai or Vietnamese. I saw lots of Southeast Asian people in the old neighborhood. Maybe he can tell me where to find a good restaurant around here. Where have all these minority kids been hiding at school?

"Next is...right. My son, Emmy. But he's not here. He works out with his school team. Joins us for all of our meets. Then we have Kotlowitz. Say hello, Mike."

"How you doin?" I'd recognize that accent anywhere. Da Region. The steel mill belt of northern Indiana, that's as much a part of Chicago as the city itself. Lots of Polish immigrants. A tough place to grow up. I wave back.

"Then we got Calvin. Calvin Sweet. He's one of our captains, along with Stefano." Calvin is a short black boy who looks like he was carved out of a block of granite. I would not want to have to wrestle him.

"Next are Don and Jako. They wrestle 152 and 160." The smaller of the boys waves. He's in a couple of my classes. Who knew?

"OK. Then we have the fearsome threesome." I hear some shuffling and laughter from the back of the group. "Knock it off, guys. Ray Harding, Dave Sperry and Jimmy Dole." The three step forward, knocking a couple of guys to the side. Oh crap! It's the guys from detention. The smokers out at the dumpster. What in the hell are they doing here? I've definitely made a mistake.

"Finally, the big boys. Ernesto Garza is our 220." A tall, light-skinned Latino guy. I've seen him hanging around with some of the football players. Hope he's not some dumb jock.

"And you know our heavyweight, Hollis. Actually the weight class is topped off at 285 pounds now."

"You gonna make weight, Hollis?" One of the smokers shouts from the back of the room.

"Dole, you want to start the practice running laps alone?" Mr. Pettus asks. "No? Then keep your mouth shut when I'm talking." The tattoo guy smirks, but says nothing more. "So that's our whole team. We are a lean fighting machine. Fourteen guys, including you, Kayla. Somebody for every weight. We should be competitive for the first time this year." Calvin and a couple of the more mature boys murmur their agreement.

"OK, let me tell you how this is gonna go. Everybody listen up, 'cause I'm not sayin' it twice. Kayla is part of this team. She doesn't get any special treatment, but I want her treated like any other wrestler—with respect. If she's going to put in the work, she's gonna get our respect. She's got our backs and we've got hers. Is that understood?" General mumbling agreement from the group.

"I've fixed her up a private changing area over there in the corner. Nobody goes over there unless she invites them. Understood? Anybody breaking that rule is off the team, no questions. Also about the Portajohn. She shares it with us now. So act like you're not a pack of wolves and keep it clean. Put the seat up when you go and then put it back down for her. And I mean clean. If I hear that it's not clean, I'm gonna randomly pick some guy to go out there and clean it. Understood?" Couple of snickers, but I think they got it. If my face isn't crimson now, it never will be.

"Other than that, we'll just practice like normal. Everybody starts with jogging. Move it." Aside to me, "Kayla, just fall in the next time around and try to follow the warm-ups. I'll ease you into it the first couple of days because you're not in shape yet." I give him a look, and he notices. "At least you're not in wrestling shape yet. OK?"

"Yes, Mr. Pettus."

"And from now on," he says firmly, "you can call me *Coach* Pettus."

I jump in between a couple of boys and take my laps around the old barn. Part of a team. A freakin' wrestling team. So this is how it starts.

CHAPTER SIXTEEN: ULYSSES RETURNS

Thursday evening after my first practice. I sit at the 1960s-era linoleum-topped kitchen table, with curving chrome legs. My eyes dart back and forth between my book and the ruled notebook I'm scribbling my homework in. That's the only way to describe my cursive writing—scribbling. June opens the creaky back door, walks to the counter and drops her heavy grocery bags with a sigh. She absentmindedly rubs her right shoulder with her left hand and looks over at me.

"Kayla, did you get supper started?"

"Not yet, I'm finishing up some…work." I stand, brush past June and dig in the cabinet under the sink for the cast iron soup pot. Hand it to June. She slams the pot down a bit too hard and starts rummaging through the pantry as cans begin to clank and roll. What's she in such a foul mood for?

"Kayla, I need a favor. I'm gonna need you to go ahead and pick up Geneva from the sitter's after school tomorrow. I'm taking Alice's closing shift at the bakery. We're not paying those late fees at the sitter again."

I turn away from June and frown. Not sure what to say, I hesitate a few seconds—hovering above the still-empty pot. "I can't do it tomorrow. I've got plans after school."

"Well, I need you to pick her up anyway. We can't afford no more time at the sitter's than we already pay for."

"But it's important," I say, trying to keep the little girl whine out of my voice.

"What have you got goin' on after school that's so important?"

I turn my back to June, focus on the pot and jiggle it mindlessly on the stove. "I don't want to talk about it. But it's important and I can't miss it."

June blows out her puffed up cheeks. I know she's staring at the back of my head. Trying to get inside it. "Why don't you just have your little friends walk with you to Sara's, pick up Geneva and then play with you here?"

"My friends aren't little and we don't *play,*" I snarl, much angrier than I intended. Soften my tone. "Besides, I'm not hanging out with friends. I told you, I'm doing something important."

"Are you meeting a boy?"

Yeah, thirteen of them. "No!" I bark, spinning on my heel to face June. "And if I were, I wouldn't tell you guys about it."

June raises her right hand to placate. "I get it. You've got your secrets. I don't expect you to tell me and Arvin every little thing that goes on in your life." June pauses for a moment and reaches in to begin emptying her brown paper grocery bag. "But just promise me that you're not drinking any beer or messing around with dope. I won't have that nonsense around my children."

"God, June, I'm not stupid. What do you..? Why do you think I would do anything so dumb? I'm just…"

"OK, OK, I just want to make it crystal clear that I won't tolerate none of that stuff around here. We got a reputation to watch after. With the church and all."

"I don't do drugs. Let it go."

"And watch that tone with me. The kids are upstairs playing. I'll be damned if I take any back sass in my own house." She is really in a mood.

Not the right time to mention you know what. June moves closer to me, crosses her arms and stares straight at my face, still thin from my crying jag and fasting last week. My face is partially covered by wisps of hair.

I turn away from her, reach under the sink and start pulling out potatoes and onions. "Sorry. It's just… I can't do it after school. I have something important to do…and I have to keep on doing it...for a while."

"Girl, like I said, we don't need to know all of your personal business. I know you're a teenager and got stuff you want to keep private." June walks to the back door, lifts the roller shade and glances into the back yard. She switches on the glaring overhead kitchen light. "But I need you to do this for me. I'm not asking you to be a full time babysitter. But once in a while, we are gonna need some help around here."

"I help out. A lot."

"I know you do, child. And Arvin and I are thankful for it." Footsteps scamper overhead and Junior screams. Then something heavy hits the floor and Denise shouts angrily.

"You two knock it off up there!" June shouts. "I didn't raise you to be a pack of wildcats!" Whispering voices, then footsteps shuffle to the top of the stairs. "Do you hear me up there?"

More whispering and then a door creaks shut. Junior's high-pitched voice calls down the stairs in sing-song, "Yes, ma'am."

June sits down at the table and rubs the bridge of her nose. I reach into the drawer for the peeler and busy myself with the potatoes, working above the nearly overflowing trash can. "Kayla, can you reach me the bottle of Bayer's?"

With my back turned to June, I drop the peeler and the potato into the sink and rummage again in the pantry. I knock several of the remaining cans on their sides before coming up with the half-full, value-sized plastic bottle of aspirin. Drop the aspirin bottle with a clatter next to June and grab a plastic drinking cup covered with smiling faces of the Hamburglar and Mayor McCheese. Then turn on the faucet and fill her glass halfway—not waiting for the tepid water to cool. I set the water down roughly beside June and a small splash wets the table and the morning newspaper. June looks up in disappointment, but I've already turned to grab the potato from the sink.

"Now I need to get this settled. Will you pick up Geneva from the sitter's tomorrow after school?"

"I told you I can't," I state sharply.

"It's not too much to ask that you help us out around here with little chores when we ask you."

"I help out plenty. And I'm not some hired hand."

"And we don't treat you like any hired hand. But you're a part of the family and the oldest. I need you to pull your weight around here."

"I didn't ask to be part of this family." I wheel around and stares daggers at June's downturned head. June's head shoots up and she is on her feet in a heartbeat. She hustles around the table and into my face.

"Listen here, girl! We took you in. We put a roof over your head. We feed you, buy your clothes. Whatever you need for school. And it ain't easy. All I'm asking is a little help in return. Is that too much to ask?"

I look down at my feet and mumble, "I didn't ask for any of this."

"I damn well know you didn't ask for what happened. But we took you in anyway."

"And where is all of my parents' money?"

June turns to face me. Looks like she's about to explode, but instead croaks out a laugh. "Money? What money?"

"My Dad made tons of money on his movies and we had…"

"Let me tell you something, girl," June says. "Your Dad was a fine actor and all, but he wasn't no business man."

"But we had…"

"Smoke and mirrors," June says, dismissively.

"What do you mean?"

"I mean your Mama and Daddy died in debt. About $160,000 worth. They was livin' off of borrowed money."

I feel a tear forming in the corner of my left eye. It slowly rolls over my cheek. I leave it there. Take three steps and jerk open the back door.

Halfway out the door, I turn to face June and shout in my most menacing tone, "I don't believe you." Step over the threshold and slam the door behind me. The door window blind clatters for several seconds as I stumble down the back steps straight into Arvin. He takes a long look at my face and holds my shoulders—at arm's length.

He says, "What's goin' on here and…"

"I want to know where my parents' money went. And…and why I'm here."

"Oh, that." He pauses for several seconds, thinking. "Let's head up and sit a while on the front porch." He takes me by my shoulder and guides me to the front of the house. Walking slowly. I don't pull away, but my shoulders and neck are stiff as a board. He pulls out two chairs from the wall and we sit side by side. Just staring at the empty street for a while.

Finally, he exhales loudly and says, "I know it's hard to hear and maybe a little hard to understand. But your Mom and Dad didn't have any money when they…when it happened."

"But how?"

"Your Dad put up a lot of his own money to

get that bear movie made. And borrowed a lot more."

"But that movie made a lot of money," I whine.

"I guess it did. But the lawyer fella said that everybody else got paid first. The studio and the bigshots and what not. I don't guess your Daddy saw much at all from that film. Just got left kind of holding the bag."

I can't believe this. I don't want to believe it.

"OK, then," I start over, "Why am I here? Why not in Chicago or…"

"OK, now that's easier to explain. Your Mom and Dad had made out a will. And that thing said that if anything would, you know, happen to both of them at the same time, they wanted you here. With family."

"But why here? Why this place?" I look at his face for the first time and see the pain. I've actually hurt an adult's feelings. I feel about two feet tall. "I didn't mean it that way, Arvin. You and June have been…"

"It's OK, girl. I know all of this has been a

shock for you. See, your Daddy and me are cousins…. were cousins. You knew that, right?" I nod. "And your Daddy used to spend summers when he was in high school down here working with me on the farm. We got along real good and had us a lot of fun. So I guess he decided…they decided that if something happened, you'd come live here with us. I'm sure they never expected it would really happen. So you're here with us. Least till you get out of high school. Then, you decide for yourself."

I stare at him long and hard. He takes out a clean handkerchief and wipes the remaining tears from my cheeks. Pats my shoulder and says, "It'll get better, girl. Just give it some time." I sit quietly for a minute, thinking. Then nod. "Now I don't know about you, but I'm ready to put the feedbag on. Something good cookin' up in there."

Arvin stands, slides the heavy dark green metal chairs back in place and opens the front door. "After you, ma'am." I exhale and walk into the house. Feel like I just ran a long race—all uphill. We walk to the kitchen and eat dinner in silence.

CHAPTER SEVENTEEN: LOVE YOU FOREVER?

After dinner last night, June pulled me aside and laid down the law. She would keep Geneva at the sitter's house until she got off work. In exchange, I am summoned to sit down with her and Arvin tomorrow night (yikes, that's tonight) to explain what I have going on after school that's so "gol darned important." So I've got a reprieve. It might only be a few hours, but it's a reprieve.

My first real practice tonight. Coach Pettus (that still sounds weird) said something about drilling yesterday. As I walk into the barn a few minutes before four, there's the same boy sitting with his back to wall, reading his book. He's my wrestling partner (whatever that means) so I better get to know him.

"Hey...my wrestling partner," I say. "Sorry, what's your name again?"

"Arthur. Arthur Boxell."

"What are you reading, Arthur Boxell?"

Arthur says, "*The Absolutely True Diary of a Part Time Indian.*"

"Is it any good?"

"Yeah, it's really good. By Sherman Alexie."

"Never heard of him."

"Really? He's one of the most famous Indian writers. American Indian. He writes a lot of stuff that's funny and kind of sad at the same time."

"What's it about?"

"An Indian kid named Arnold who decides to go to an all-Anglo school. I think you could relate to him."

"I'm like an Indian boy named Arnold?" Arthur laughs. He's got a good sense of humor.

"No, I mean he's in kind of a similar situation to you. New kid, at a strange school, in a strange town, doesn't know anybody, trying to figure out how he fits in." How does he know all of this? I sometimes forget. This is Felton. Bad news travels fast.

"How does he fit in? Maybe I can take a few pointers from him."

"He joins a sports team."

"You're joking me."

"No, really."

"Don't tell me he's a wrestler," I say. Arthur laughs again.

"No. No wrestling. Couple of fights, though." He looks up at me and smiles. He's probably heard about Donnie and me. "No, he's a basketball player."

"And does it help him fit in?" I'm intrigued

"Yeah, it does. But he's still got a sad life. At home and stuff."

"I can relate."

"You can borrow it when I'm finished. If you want. I got another Alexie book at home. Called *The Lone Ranger and Tonto Fistfight in Heaven*." He looks up and smiles again. I think we're gonna get along.

"Is that really the title?"

"It's really the title. He's a funny guy."

"Are you Native American?"

"We prefer our tribal name. I'm a Miami. We didn't exactly agree to the 'being American' thing." I nod.

Coach Pettus walks in. The whistle blows and people get serious really fast. I learn what drilling is. Doing the same thing over and over and over again. Even after you're bored with doing it and tired. Takedowns today. Escapes on Monday. Whatever an escape is. At the end of practice, Coach Pettus calls me over.

"You did a good job for your first day. You pay attention and you learn from your mistakes."

"Arthur helped me a lot."

"He's a good kid. Very calm and patient. That's an asset for a wrestler. I've got a form that you need June and Arvin to sign. Giving you permission to compete on the team. You've talked to them, right?" I hesitate, then shake my head no. "OK, you need to get on that. Have them sign the form and get it back to me on Monday. And try to do some running over the weekend. To work on your stamina. Six minutes will seem like forever during a match if you're not in good condition. We'll do some stuff in practice to build up your endurance. But you need to do some work outside practice as well. OK?"

"OK Mr...I mean Coach Pettus. Any advice

on how to break this to them?"

"Just tell them what you're doing and why you're doing it. If they have any questions, just have them call me. Goodnight, Kayla."

"Goodnight, Coach." I'm not sure why I'm doing this. How am I gonna explain that to June and Arvin? Better think of something—fast.

Dinner, or supper as it's called around here, is grilled cheese sandwiches and some soup. Not many dishes involved, but I volunteer to clean up. More time to stall. Just as I wipe off the kitchen table for about the fourth time, June calls.

"Kayla, can you come in to the parlor? To talk to me and Arvin?" This is it. Go time. As I walk into the front room, I see that June has arranged the chairs. She and Arvin on one side and the defendant (that's me) on the other. I take a deep breath and look up.

June starts. "So we need to know what's going on. What's so all-fired important at school that you can't bring Geneva home from the sitter's?"

"It's not at school."

"Where, then?" That's the wrong question.

"I'm …I'm trying something new."

"We figured that," Arvin offers. "But we can't puzzle out what this 'something' is."

"I joined the wrestling team." A full eight seconds of stunned silence. I counted.

Then June says, "You never. Now what's really goin' on? Stop messin' around."

"I'm not joking. I joined the team. We practice every day after school."

"They don't let no girl on a wrestling team," June mocks, a small smile playing at the edge of her mouth.

"Yeah, they do," I say, defensively. "In fact, they invited me to join. They need me."

June turns to Arvin. "Is this girl being serious?"

Like a light bulb pops up over Arvin's head, he looks up. "Ohhh. Is this Emerson's club? The one where he helps out those boys?"

"Yes. Coach Pettus invited me to join and…"

June cuts me off. "Well, I'm sayin' 'no'. We're not gonna have no girls in this house grabbin' and gropin' around with a bunch of boys.

It's not right. No ma'am. Not one bit lady-like."

"I don't want to be a *lady.* "

June laughs. "Well, girl, that's the way God made you, and you sure can't change things." I roll my eyes. No sense arguing about that.

"I'm doing it anyway. There's nothing wrong with it and …"

"Nothing wrong with it? Nothing wrong with it?" June gets a lot louder when she repeats things. "I'll tell you what's wrong with it. I'm not gonna have the people of this town and our church and what not thinking that we're all living in sin over here. No ma'am. Not on my watch and…"

Arvin cuts her off. He can see where this is headed and tries to take it down a notch. "Now, June. Why don't you let me call Emerson and see if I can straighten this out. I'll just…"

June jumps out of her chair. Knocks it back into the end table behind her. Both the table lamp and glass of tea on table top sway ominously. Arvin half stands, and steadies the lamp and glass with both hands, before they hit the ground. June stomps into the kitchen and we hear a lot of banging. Arvin puts his fingers in his ears and I smile—briefly. Ten seconds later, I smell smoke. She's having a cigarette. Right in the house! As far as I know, she hasn't had a cigarette since just after I arrived last spring. Arvin looks over and shrugs. He says, "I'll be right back," and walks out. He dials the rotary phone and I hear one side of a quiet conversation.

I let myself out to the front porch. Plop down in the swing and move gently. I'm not going to take up smoking, but I need some fresh air. Drop my head on the swing back and look up at the stars. They are really pretty here. Haven't really noticed them before. You almost never see stars in Chicago. Even on a clear night. I wonder if there's a girl on some other planet going through the same things I am? I hope she's handling it better. Good luck, sister. I sit for about ten minutes. Then the door opens. Arvin first. Wearing his stained brown Carhartt jacket. June wears a light blue sweater with a white lace collar, pulled over her shoulders. She throws me a Felton Warriors sweatshirt.

"Thanks," I say. June doesn't respond. Arvin motions to the swing and I scoot over, making room for him. He sits with a loud sigh.

June pulls up the fading green chair and sits at an angle to my side. No more head-on confrontation. It's better that way.

Arvin starts, "I just got off the phone with Emerson and everything the girl says is true."

"But I still don't…"

"June, would you let me finish?" June glares at Arvin. "Please?" She waves him away like an old mare swatting a gnat with its tail.

"Like I said, Emerson is backing her up. He invited her to join. Thinks she can be pretty good. He's seen her work. She's strong and balanced…and smart. Emerson says that's more important for a wrestler than most people know." I say nothing, but this makes me feel good. Coach has my back.

Arvin continues. "He says there aren't too many girls in wrestling, but there are a few. A lot of them are daughters of the coaches. Some of them turn out to be really good. They've got their own motivation." Arvin pauses to let his words sink in. June sits back and looks away, like she's lost in another world. "But Emerson did say something else. Said the matches are not gonna be easy. Not just the physical stuff. Kayla's gonna hear some comments. Mean things. Some downright nasty and crude talk. Think you could handle that, girl?" June looks up. That got her attention.

"Yeah, I can handle it." I hear stuff like that all the time at school. And all I did there was show up as the new kid. I can ignore stupid people's comments.

Arvin looks over at June and she stares back at him. For a long time. Finally she breaks the silence. "Kayla, can you go in and get Geneva ready for bed? Let me talk to Arvin for a minute?"

I'll do that in a heartbeat. "Yes, ma'am." I'm up and out of there in the blink of an eye. Bound up the stairs and into the nursery, or whatever you call a four-year-old's room. Geneva is sitting on the floor. Her pull-up is on backward and she has one foot through the armhole of her one-piece pajamas with smiling purple Barneys all over them.

"C'mere, you shrimp," I tease, grabbing her around her chubby tummy.

She squeals and says, "I'm no shrimp.

You're the shrimp."

"No, *you're* the shrimp," I tease.

"No *YOU'RE* the shrimp." This could go on forever.

"Let me get your pull-up turned around, and I'll read you a bedtime story. OK?"

She nods, wobbling her head around until she laughs. "Which one do you want?"

"*Love You Forever*?" she asks, softly. "But you don't have to read it if it makes you sad again." Wow, this kid's perceptive for a four-year-old.

"No, I'll read it. I like that book. My Mom used to read it to me and …" All of a sudden I've got tears popping out of both eyes. I wipe both sides of my face, fish the book out of a jumble of her toys and settle her down in my lap.

She turns and looks up at me—all serious. "Kayla, do you miss your Mommy and Daddy?" More tears. I can't stop them. Nod my head.

"But you'll get to see them again…in heaven. They're waiting for you."

"Yeah, but…" I stop. I'm talking to a little girl.

"Kayla?" She looks up at me with huge

brown eyes. "I'll be your family. Until you go to see your Mommy and Daddy again." I hug her tight to my chest. Now there's a waterworks. A flood. A downpour. But no sound. Hold her close, until I see a shadow at the door. June glides in slowly. Gently takes Geneva out of my arms, and says, "OK, Missy, time for you to get to bed." With Geneva's head draped over her shoulder, June turns to face with me with a look of…is that sadness? Sympathy? She motions me to go downstairs. Arvin is sitting in the kitchen, blowing into his coffee. Re-reading the morning paper. He doesn't look up.

"Well, girl, I guess you can keep on with the wrestling. June isn't all that excited about it, but she'll come around. She don't like things to change. At least not too fast. Makes her kind of nervous. Like the world won't ever be the same anymore."

I can relate to that. I've seen enough change in the last six months to last a lifetime. I just want to get on with my life. I stand and pat Arvin on the shoulder. He reaches up and touches my hand. Very briefly. It's the first time I've touched his calloused hand since I moved here.   Maybe things are   changing   again.

CHAPTER EIGHTEEN: TRIP TO VANITY FAIR

It's been two days at home since my big announcement. And it's been quiet around here. Pin-drop quiet. Eerily quiet. Arvin has been off on a big construction project. Junior and Denise haven't been looking for ways to torment me. At least they haven't carried out any of their devious plans since Friday. The little sweetie came by a couple of times, held my hand and smiled up at me. Sometimes I think of her as the angel in the house. Like Beth in *Little Women*. I can't think that way though. That would be more than I could bear. But even Geneva's been closed-mouthed the last couple of days. When June hasn't been working, she just shuffles by me without a word. Not angry or anything. Just all business. It's like something's in the air. Some fairies are flying around stealing everyone's voices.

Once again, I'm not complaining. No

talking means no hassles. I got out and ran on Saturday. Just like the coach instructed. Went three whole miles on a lonely country road without stopping. Actually about a mile and half out, quick drink from my bottle, then right back home. I was kind of proud of myself. I've never run that far before. Today I did sprints. Through the rows of a cornfield owned by a friend of Arvin's. No chance of a run-in with a tractor there. The corn's all harvested. Twenty times up and down the rows. Till I got good and winded. Actually broke a decent sweat.

Mom used to tell me that women don't sweat. They glow. Well, Mom, if you were here now, you'd see your girl all sweated out. If you were here. If you hadn't been looking at your damn phone. Why did you do that? It's so stupid and pointless. Makes me furious.

About three o'clock, I'm in the middle of homework and June breaks the silence. "Grab your jacket, girl. We're goin' into town."

Over the past six months, I've learned a little of the local vernacular. I know that 'town' means Sheffield. Now if she had said 'the city,' that would be Indianapolis. But since I haven't been to 'the city' since we drove through it last April on the way from Chicago, I'm pretty sure we're headed to Sheffield. We drive up through Felton. Most businesses are closed on Sunday, but a few people stroll the few blocks that have sidewalks. June waves and says "Hey" to several people along the way. Some are just getting out of church, still dressed up in their Sunday clothes. People really take their church stuff seriously around here. June has asked me to go with them several times, but I have an excuse every time. That's one more battle I need to put off as long as possible.

We drive north along cornfield-lined county roads, with barely enough room for two cars to pass. Nobody seems to care. Both cars slow down, both drivers check to see who the other person is and both drivers wave politely—whether they know the other driver or not. At first I thought it was kind of weird. Now I just…I'm not sure if I think it's cool, but at least I'm used to it. Guess you can get used to a lot of strange stuff.

We roll into the edge of town. The big

town. I know we're there because I see the sign: *Sheffield, City of Progress.* That works for me. I'm a pretty progressive girl. I wonder whether Sheffield's idea of progress is the same as mine? I'll be sure to ask the mayor, next time I see her. On our right is an old drive-in theater. The sign says *Skylight Drive-in.* In big red, swirly neon letters. The 'R' on the sign is burned out, so it's just a "dive-in" now. I'm sure the locals find that funny. On the marquee where they put the name of the movies, the sign reads "Closed for the winter. Come back and see us in May!" Yep, I'll be sure to put that into my calendar.

June drives slowly through the seven or eight blocks to the center of the town. I know they call the center 'the square.' I've heard kids at school say "I'll meet you at 'the square.'" But that's a pretty bizarre name, because the center of town is clearly a circle. I'll be sure to bring that up with the mayor too. Halfway around the circle and I catch my breath. That statue. The boy holding the two bear cubs. Up high on a pedestal, ten feet above me. All dark green from the weather. I turn and stare at the statue through the back window as we drive past. I ask June to drive around the circle once again. She does so without a word. There's nobody else on the circle, so she crawls to a stop in front of the thing, the second time around.

"Do you want to get out?"

"No." I'm crying. Just a little, but I'm crying. June says nothing, but reaches into the glove box and hands me a package of tissues. I pull one out and dry my eyes. One final look up at the boy and his cubs before we pull slowly away. It's Dad's statue. Not his personally, but from his movie. The famous one. He played the father of the boy on the statue. Everybody knows about the movie. All over the country. But how many people know about this statue? And why it's here? In this town? Not many I'd guess. And nobody knows that the daughter of the famous John Burbadge is driving around the town today, sniffling into some tiny tissues. Nobody knows me. Nobody wants to know me.

June pulls around the circle and makes the next right, onto Harrison Street. Past the banks, the shoe store and a fancy ladies' clothing store. Fancy for Sheffield anyway. Two blocks more and she turns right again. Pulling into one of several open parking spaces in the first block. People in Chicago would kill for this kind of parking. Parking in Chicago is like a competitive sport. No, it's more Darwinian. It's survival of the fittest. Or the fastest or the one who knows the neighborhood best. Or the one who can squeeze their car into the smallest space. Dad was always proud that he could wedge our car into parking spaces that others would drive away from. My Dad. Daddy.

"C'mon, girl, let's go." June is out the door and headed for an alley. I jump out and follow behind like a little puppy. I have no idea where we're going. June walks past several doors and stops beside a dirty white one. At least I think it was white many years ago. It's not really in anybody's color palette now. June pulls out a circle of keys and fishes around. Finds the key she's looking for and sticks it into the lock on the dirty door. It won't turn and she shakes her head. Drops her bag to the ground and grabs the top of the door with her other hand. Simultaneously, she kicks the bottom of the door while pushing at the top. The lock spins to the left and the door opens.

A symphony of smells assaults my nose. First is a sickly sweet smell. Then flour mixed with the smell of vanilla, cherry and a few other scents I can't make out. It feels like I'm sticking my head into a vat of cotton candy. The room is dimly lit and the fading afternoon light from the alley spills into the top of the room. Repetitive scratching noises come from the far side of the room. Somewhere near the floor. June ignores the noises, walking up a small ramp. The puppy (me) creeps along behind her. She reaches up and pulls a string. The room ahead is flooded with florescent light. June walks into the room past long tables with butcher block tops. Each table is spotlessly clean, but heavily worn—like they've been used for decades. On my right are a mountain of bowls, pans, trays and spoons of varying sizes. Tools I don't recognize. Ahead, there's enormous machinery, like in a factory. As we move out of the lighted area and into shadow again, the scratching sounds get louder. Then louder still. Beneath the scratching is the faint sound of music. I can almost make out the song. Almost.

June reaches for another light string and

pulls. Three feet in front of us, a boy is on the floor. On his hands and knees, with some kind of tool in his hands—a scraper. He jumps slightly when the second light goes on.

"Oh hey, Rick," June offers, casually. "What you doin' workin' on a Sunday?"

The boy pulls his earbuds out. The song gets a little louder. Some Katy Perry thing. Great choice. Or not.

"Hey there, June." The boy is short with dark hair. Built like a mini-weightlifter. Probably a little older than me. He stares at me curiously. "We had practice yesterday. Dad hasn't gotten any new help yet for the winter, so I'm doin' pans and floors today."

"Kind of early to start Saturday practices."

"Yeah, but we're goin' all out this year. Some of us are aimin' for States." The boy stares at me like I'm a circus animal. I stare back. I'm not the one on my knees on some dirty floor. Takes a while, but finally June notices.

"Rick, this is Kayla. She's...she lives with us now. Kayla, this is Rick. Rick Gray. His dad owns this place." Duh, so we're in the bakery where June works. In the back. Where they actually bake the stuff. Never seen one of these places before. The boy shows me his dirty hand and just waves. No smile. Not overly friendly.

"We'll let you get back to work. Good luck this year." The boy pops his buds back in and resumes his scraping. June keeps walking and eventually I follow her. It's clear this kid's got nothing to say to me. We walk past a large storage area loaded with tall, empty aluminum racks. About six feet high. June pushes a rack out of her way and walks into the front. We are behind the counter of Gray's Bakery. Feels weird to be in here with all the lights off. June wanders among the display cases until she finds the one she wants. Pulls out a pan of brownies and starts loading some into a white paper tray.

"Are you sure we should be here?" I mumble, picturing the cops busting in at any minute. June waves away my question.

"I got a key to the back door and I let myself in here every day to work." As if that explains everything.

"But isn't this like…stealing."

June looks up and smirks. "No, it's not stealing. I pay for everything I take. Reduced rate 'cause I work here." She fishes in her purse, opens the cash register and drops in a few singles. "I promised the kids some brownies, so we're just pickin' them up on our way to the errands." She hands me a brownie and I take a bite. Wow, that's good. I take another taste.

"What errands?" I ask. I'm not crazy about wild goose chases.

"Well, I don't have to like this rasslin' thing. But I'm gonna make sure you go out there lookin' decent. Emerson told Arvin what you need, so we'll get it at the Walmart. He figures you need some of them compression shorts and a couple sports bras, or whatever they call them." She eyes my upper body, then looks away.

So that's what this mystery trip is all about. She's actually helping me get ready for wrestling.

"And one more thing we need to get. You don't have to cut your hair short like some boy to wrestle. But you need one of those things to get your hair out of the way. Not sure what they're called. Like a tight hair net. I don't want to see none of them boys cheatin' and trying to pull your hair." Rick must be listening, because he laughs quickly, then catches himself.

"I called over to the Walmart. They got the other stuff, but not the hair thing. So Griff got it in special from the city. Said he never ordered one of them before." I have no idea who Griff is.

She looks at her watch and pushes the cash register closed. "We got to get movin'. Griff's meeting us special." We make our way quickly back the way we came. June waves at Rick, who nods in return. He doesn't even glance at me. Nice to meet you too, dude. She turns out lights on the way out, locks up the dirty back door and we walk quickly back to the car. Nearly dark now.

We drive two blocks back in the direction we came and park in front of a dark storefront. *Griff's Sporting Goods.* Written on a handmade sign. June motions me to stay in the car. She walks quickly up and a tall older man meets her at the doorway to the store. They smile at each other, hug and share a few words. Seems like they are old friends. He hands June a brown paper bag, and she fishes in her purse for money. The man gently pushes her purse away and June seems to insist. The man says a few more words and points to the car—directly at me. He smiles and waves in my direction—like somebody's grandpa. I wave back weakly. I... don't...know this guy? June pats the old man on the back, and he turns and steps unsteadily into the dark store. June turns away slowly. Looks back once more, sadly. Then starts for the car. She tosses the paper bag in my direction. I'm not ready and the bag bounces off my chest onto the floor.

Before she starts the car, June glances in my direction. "Griff ordered that special on Friday night. Came on down and opened up his store for us tonight. Then wouldn't take no money for it. Says you been through enough. Need a break here." She looks away and back toward the dark store. The smallest hint of a smile. A sad smile, just the same.

"Go on, girl, open it up."

I pull open the paper bag and rip the plastic off the item inside. Out falls an elasticized, nylon hat-looking thing. Stretchy and tight. Electric pink with black lightning bolts criss-crossing the thing.

It's kind of freaky. But cool.

"I picked out this pattern special. If you're gonna be out there rasslin' all them boys, you're not gonna let 'em forget you're a girl." June stares at me with a serious expression. "Is that OK by you?"

I look over at her wrinkled face and nod. Damn straight it's OK with me.

CHAPTER NINETEEN: THE TASTE OF LOVE MEDICINE

Monday afternoon. Two forty. Exactly thirty minutes till school lets out. Then fifty minutes until wrestling practice. Fifty minutes to get dressed for practice and ride to the barn. For a two-hour practice, including a couple of five-minute breaks. At the end of practice we may wrestle live. That's three two-minute periods with zero breaks in between. I have now managed to convince myself that math is, in fact, useful in life. And killed five minutes. Now it's two forty-five and ...

Walking to my locker, a tight knot of girls brushes by. Following close on the heels of Madison, Raven and some other cheerleader. One of the girls hits my elbow and my books go flying. Madison, Raven and the group look back and a snicker starts in the center, then radiates out to the fringes until a chorus of laughter fills the halls. Raven spins to leave and the rest follow. Like sheep following a shepherd.   Some shepherd.

    I bend to pick up my books and another student appears by my side. Seemingly out of nowhere. A tall girl with long, reddish brown hair. Picks up three of my books and hands them to me without a word. Smiles and walk off, turning the corner and rounding into the C hallway. Are there really a couple of decent kids in this school? Will wonders never cease?

    Entering the wrestling room (OK it's a wrestling barn), hammering and sawing fills the air. The waft of sawdust takes me back to trips to the Crafty Badger hardware store on Saturday mornings with Dad. He wasn't much of a handyman. I think he just liked shooting the breeze with the owner's son, Harry, and some of the other guys that worked in the back. They were always good for a funny story about some building project gone wrong. They were always talking about some doofus or another. Always good for a laugh.

    Above the wrestling mat, the old hay loft has been removed and the frame of an upper level balcony has been installed. I see Arvin, up on scaffolding, working away with a hammer. He glances down and waves, but continues his hammering. So this is where he's been all weekend. Nobody tells me anything. Just past Arvin is the woman from the furniture store in Felton. She looks at some kind of plan on a large rolled up paper. Takes a measurement and marks a board with flat pencil she pulls from behind her ear. Hands the board to a third man (one that I've never seen before) and he starts to saw on her mark.

Arthur walks up and drops his bag near my feet. He holds a book with dog-eared pages. Without my asking, he holds it up so I can read the title—*Love Medicine* by Louise Erdrich. It's like he can read my mind.

"Yes, it's a good book. Actually a great book. A classic. By an Indian author. A *woman* Indian author. And yes, you can borrow it when I'm done."

I've heard it said that people who spend a lot of time together can start to guess what the other person is thinking. Finish each other's sentences. If that's the case, Arthur Boxell and I are going to be communicating without talking before this season is over. We're inseparable in the wrestling room.

That's how it is with workout partners.

I ask, "What are they doing up there?"

"Making some kind of a seating area."

"Seating for what?"

"For when we start having matches in here. Real home matches."

"You've never had home matches before?"

"Nope. This is my third year. First year in this barn. And every match has been on the road. In somebody else's gym. In front of the all the other team's fans. The guys are getting tired of not having people support them."

"So," I muse, "if you build it, they will come?"

"That's the plan anyway," Arthur says, smiling. "Not sure if many people at Felton even know we have a wrestling team. We're pretty low profile at this school. In fact, we're pretty close to no profile."

"How do we change that?"

"Maybe you'll be the one that changes things." Arthur chuckles to himself. An inside joke I guess.

"What do you mean?"

"Well, some people might come out to see if a girl can really wrestle with the boys."

"You mean come out to see me get pounded. I know a couple of people who would pay good money for that." I snort a quick laugh. Arthur laughs with me this time.

"You're gonna do fine. You've picked up a lot in just a few days. And besides, look who you got for a teacher." Arthur motions to himself with a magician's flourish.

A whistle blows and Calvin starts to jog around the edge of the mat. A couple other guys fall in behind him. Arthur and I join the circle and work our way around and around and around the mat. After our jogging comes stretching. Then some crazy wrestling-related warmups. At least it seemed crazy last week. Now I'm starting to get used to it. Bridges to build up our neck muscles. Leg tosses to build up our core muscles. Speed and agility drills. Hopping over lines—first one leg, then the other. Forward and back, then side to side. Then two legs. Then back to one. Working on our stances. For when we wrestle on our feet. High stance, then low stance. Side to side. Forward and back again. To fake the other guy out and take them down to the mat. Under control. Two points for the top man. I'm starting to get the hang of this sport. And I don't cringe about calling myself the top *man*. Some things are not worth arguing about.

Coach Pettus strides in and blows his whistle. I still can't get used to that wild prosthetic. All curved and gleaming. The oddest shade of orange. Like a bright orange sunset swirled with browns and reds. It must have been designed by an artist.

"Alright guys. Drill time. We're going to work on bottom today. Escapes and reversals."

I move to a far corner of the mat, but Arthur motions me to follow him.

"Why?" I whisper under my breath. Arthur looks at me and jerks his head to the other side of the mat. He seems insistent. He takes a few steps toward the far side of the mat and I follow.

"I forgot my headgear." He shakes his head no, but I run to pick it up. In the corner where we came from. As I reach to pick up my dark blue, shiny headgear, the big guys, Dole and Sperry stare in my direction.

Just loud enough for me to hear, Dole whispers, "You can run, but you can't hide." Hollis steps forward and stands between the boys and me. Doesn't say a word. Doesn't move a muscle. Just stands there. I nod at him, grab my headgear and sprint to the other side of the mat, where Arthur stands looking disappointed.

When coach calls for a five-minute water break or a "rinse out" (whatever that means), I pull Arthur to the corner on our edge of the mat.

"What was that all about?" I ask.

"What was what?"

"At the beginning of practice. Why did we have to move down here?"

"It's those guys." He motions toward the far end of the mat. "Those guys. It's ... Dole and Sperry. And their buddy Harding, too. They're bad guys." I look at him skeptically. "No, Kayla, they're really bad guys. You need to stay away from them. They're not from here and they…"

"I'm not from around here either. So what?"

"Just believe me, Kayla. Stay as far away from them as you can. I've seen what they do and..."

Coach blows his whistle and practice resumes. Stand ups and switches and rolls and sit outs and Petersons. Who knew there were so many ways to get away from somebody trying to hold you down? New scoring information today too. New for me, anyway. Two points for switching positions from underneath a guy to top of the guy. It's good to be top dog. And one point for escaping his control. Then try to take him down again. I'm getting the hang of this. Coach shows us a funky way to get free of the other guy's grip. Shows us how to get just under his fingertips, grab four of his fingers in a crushing grip and hold them away from our body until we are out. It hurts like anything when Arthur does it to me. Must hurt him too, because he shakes out his fingers after I do the hold on him. That's one to remember.

There's no clock in our wrestling room wall, so no distractions. Practice is over when Coach says it's over. Finally, Coach says it's over. He asks everybody to stick around for a few minutes. I drop my cup of water in the trash and take a seat. On the opposite side of Coach Pettus from the big guys. Maybe Arthur knows something.

"First, I want to say that I like your intensity level. Everybody in this room is working hard. That work's gonna show up during matches. For you newcomers, I guess that's just Hollis and Kayla…"

"And me, Coach."

"Right, sorry Don. You too. Anyway, new people, this is just the beginning. Practices are going to get harder and longer as the season progresses. We're just getting you into shape right now. Wrestling shape, that is. It's different from football shape or cross country shape. Those sports tend to be aerobic. Our sports is anaerobic. That means that you are going to have shorts bursts of extreme intensity in a match. You're gonna get tired out there. But you're gonna keep on wrestling after you're exhausted. After you think you can't go on. 'Cause let me tell you a secret. You can and will go on. Six minutes is a long time alone on a wrestling mat."

Murmurs of assent from the team. I hadn't thought that I'll be all alone out there for six minutes. There are always the other guys in practice. Arthur's there to help me. But not in a match. I'll be all alone. Just me, myself and I. Oy vey.

"The older guys will tell you. It's a long time. So you've got to train outside practice to get in the best physical shape you can. We've talked about running. Some distance work, some sprints, combine them both sometimes. Mix it up. But I also want you doing sit ups, pull ups, leg lifts, core work, lifting. And strengthen those hands! They are two of your most valuable weapons in a match. Get yourself one of those hand grippers at Walmart or someplace. Doesn't have to be expensive. But use the thing. While you're watching TV, getting on Facebook or talking on the phone with your girlfriend." A few chuckles from the team. "Or your boyfriend, Kayla." The Coach smiles. My face is beet red, but I look back at him and shake my head.

"I know you've all seen the construction here in the barn. But don't get your hopes up. We're not gonna be done in time to have a home meet this year. Next year for sure, though. I've got the schedule pretty well set. We've got thirteen matches."

Someone in the back says "Oooooo."

"I know, right? Lucky thirteen. Anyway, everything is on the road again. Just like last year. So we've got to fit our matches, which you guys know are technically exhibitions. They don't count on the other teams' records. We have to fit into their schedules. When they can work us into their gyms. You veterans will know most of the teams. The usual suspects. Garner, Edinboro, Kingsport, Green Ridge, Morrisville, Rushton, Bartsville...who am I forgetting?"

"Sheffield, Coach?" Stefano asks softly from beside him.

"Right, thanks Mendez. Yeah, Sheffield will be our last match." A couple of guys groan. "Not ideal, I know. But we'll be ready for them. Hey, don't believe everything you hear. The rankings don't mean anything. Sheffield is just a bunch of guys like us. They put on their pants one leg at a time in the morning." He looks over at me.

I hesitate for one beat then blurt out, "Yeah, I do it that way, too."

Coach Pettus smiles and continues, "Yep,

that's what I figured. Anyway, we're gonna take every match seriously; we respect all of our opponents. Don't take anybody for granted. But we're gonna demand respect from them too. And that includes Sheffield. First match is in two weeks. At Garner. Younger guys work out rides with the older guys. OK, everybody with me?" Heads nod and guys chant "yes." "Alright then. Break it down on the captains."

Calvin and Stefano get down in the referee's position. On their hands and knees. We all crowd around them and everybody puts one hand on their backs. From underneath, Calvin shouts in a deep loud voice, "OK, Felton pride on three! One, two, three!"

They entire team shouts in unison "Felton Pride!" And just like that, practice is over.

Hollis offers me a ride home and for once, I accept. I've got my headlamp from Chicago, but it's cold out and I'm tired. Bone tired. We drive the dark country roads. No talking, but he hums a popular song. Repeats the chorus over and over. "Summer time in Northern Michigan." I think we're going to have a lot more winter here before we see summer again.

Hollis pulls up the drive and crunches to a stop on the gravel. Jumps out before I can stop him, grabs my bike and wheels it under the back porch. Safe from the rain and snow and sleet and whatever. He continues whistling the song and waves goodbye as he climbs into the truck. Backs the truck a couple of feet, stops and pokes his head out the window.

"Kayla. Pay attention to what Arthur says. He knows."

I look at him—puzzled. He nods toward me and rolls out of the drive. I walk to the shed and grab the big bag of dog food. Doesn't feel so heavy anymore. I march straight up to the dogs and undo the chains from their collars. They sit at my feet and wait patiently to be fed. I pour their food and lean against one of the dog houses as they eat below me.

I look up at the sky and wonder. Why did you do it? You always told me that texting and driving don't mix. And I was only thirteen! Three years until my first license. But I remember that. It just makes me so damn angry that she would do something so stupid. Sometimes I just…I just hate…NO! I can't think this way. I won't think this way. You also taught me to forgive and move on. Oh, I do forgive you. I do. I love you Mommy and Daddy. I always will. I stare at the night sky, the big dipper straight overhead.

Are you out there somewhere?

Can you see me?

Do   you   still   love   me?

CHAPTER TWENTY: A FRIEND IS ONE WHO KNOWS YOU

Nearly every student groans as Mr. Chenoweth explains the assignment. I'm not one of them. Not a groaner, I mean.

"You're each going to write a sonnet. Just like Shakespeare did. You all know Shakespeare right? Maybe you've seen Clare Danes and Leonardo DeCaprio in *Romeo and Juliet?* The modern remake? It was few years ago and took place in a beach town in California."

Pretty much nobody responds. I nod my head, just a little, when he looks my way.

"Shakespeare was a pretty famous writer," he says. "Actually the most famous writer in the Western world. But he wasn't as well known when he wrote his plays. Not like a big star today. Not like Johnny Depp or Ben Affleck or ...Yes, Kayla?"

"Or Emma Watson or Gabby Sidibe," I say

"Right. Kayla brings up a great point. Not

all famous actors are white American men."

"Just the ones I'd like to date," Madison says under her breath, and the students around her snicker. I'm not one of them.

"Anyway, back to Shakespeare. You all know he wrote some famous plays. Who can name one?"

Not one hand goes up. Really. Not one. Can nobody in this class name a Shakespeare play? Or do they think he's too boring and uncool? I don't think either thing, and my hand goes up.

"Kayla, I expect you would have some inside knowledge on that. Name a couple. Your favorites."

I think for a few seconds. "*Macbeth*. For a tragedy. For a comedy probably… let's see…either *Twelfth Night* or *Midsummer Night's Dream*."

"Good choices. Have you read any of his histories?"

That one's easy. "*Henry the IV, Part 2*. I like how Hal grows up. Takes responsibility for his own life." Madison and Raven glare at me like I just told them I plan to murder their kittens. And said it in Swahili. They look at me like I'm nuts.

From another planet. I can stare back too, girls.

"Thanks for starting us out, Kayla. In addition to his wonderful plays, Shakespeare also wrote poetry. Beautiful poetry." More groans, mostly from the boys. "A very precise and exact type of poetry called a sonnet. Over the next couple of weeks, we're going to learn how a sonnet is constructed. What makes a sonnet a sonnet and not some other type of poem. Then I'm going to turn you all loose to write your own sonnets and …."

Most of the class misses the end of his sentence, because they bolt out the door for lunch. I hear the end though.

"…you're going to work in teams to help each other write your sonnets."

Can't wait to see which loser I get paired up with. Should be loads of fun. Loads. Grab my brown paper lunch bag from the top of my backpack and head outside. When I get to the glass double doors leading to the athletic fields, I hear a crash and jump. It's snowing outside. Snowing hard. Crazy, right? What is it—November 10th? And in the middle of this snowstorm there is thunder and lightning. We're having a freaking thundersnow! Guess I can cancel my lonely little picnic at the baseball diamond. This time it's for real. I've got to face the hoards.

Turn into the lunch room and head for the line to buy an apple. Up ahead are Donnie and Todd and they are holding up the line. Saying something to one of the lunch ladies. A heavy woman in a white hair net. Maybe in her forties, but she looks much older. I can't hear what they are saying, but I can see her reaction. She looks scared and is red in the face. Like she can't believe what she's hearing. She stares at them and listens. Says nothing in return. They finally tire of their game and move on. The line moves ahead slowly.

By the time I get to the lunch lady, I can see she's crying. Tears on both cheeks. But she doesn't stop working. Keeps on shoveling food to these kids who don't even see her. Have no idea how she's feeling. And don't care.

"May I have an apple, please?"

She sniffles and picks one out. "Is this one OK, sweetheart?"

"It's fine. Thanks." I start to move on and then take a step back. Lean over the counter and speak to her quietly. "Ignore whatever those guys said to you. They're just jerks. Bullies who like to get under people's skin and…"

"Thanks, Kayla." She knows my name. The lunch lady who I've never seen before knows my name. "I know they're just dumb kids showing off. And most days I can ignore it. But today it just got to me. My boy's home sick, but I got to come in here and work. I haven't had much sleep and …" Some kid behind me yells over at me to "Move it." I glare at him and return to the lady.

"But just try to ignore them. If they said stuff to me I'd spit in their food, but…" She laughs and I wave goodbye. She returns to shoveling hot dogs and beans onto kids' trays.

I step into the maelstrom of the lunchroom, and it's like walking into the center of a massive storm. It's loud in here. I mean deafening. Every once in a while, some food goes flying. The lone lunchroom monitor tries to find the kids throwing food. But no one will point them out. It's like the food magically flies from one table to another. I stick to the side of the room and make my way in. Almost to the other side, with no offers to sit down.

Big surprise. Then, I hear my name.

"Kayla. Hey, Kayla." It's Hollis. One table over from the wall. The table is full, but he motions me to join them. Stands and grabs an empty chair from the table behind him. Nobody challenges him. He's a pretty big guy. Clears off space at the end of the table. I pull out the chair to sit and there's Bao sitting to Hollis' right. Next to him is Arthur. On the other side is Calvin and Mike Kotlowitz, the boy from up by Chicago. Sitting beside Mike is the red-haired girl who helped me pick up my books. Who is she? I sit for a couple of seconds, then open my sandwich bag. For some reason, look over and see a girl sitting alone. On the floor. In a corner. Ignored by everyone in this place.

I jump up. "Be right back," I say to no one and everyone. The girl doesn't see me as I approach. Her head is down and her hair covers her face. But I know who she is. "Hi, Kenna Faye. You're back." Duh, of course she's back. She's sitting right here.

I haven't seen Kenna Faye smile many times. And never in the couple of weeks before she left. But she seems glad to see me. "Hey, Kayla.

Long time, no see," she says. "Long time, nobody see. Me that is."

"You're back," I repeat. Really? Again?

"It would seem so. Present and accounted for. In the flesh. Reporting for duty."

"I'm so glad to see you. I've been so worried and I didn't hear anything and I was …" She stops me.

"I'm fine. And I'm back. And I'm…it's good to see you too. But you should get back to your friends and …" My turn to cut her off.

"No. You're gonna sit with us too. It's just the guys. The wrestlers and … "

"I know who they are. What I don't know is why you're sitting with them."

"Right. You haven't heard. I kind of…I joined the wrestling team. I'm a wrestler."

"You're a what?"

I laugh. "I'm a wrestler." It's weird to say it out loud. But it makes me feel something. Proud, maybe?

Kenna Faye says, "You're not joking."

I cross my heart. "Dead serious. So come over and join us." I grab her metal Beatles lunch box and help her up. I'm not taking 'no' for an answer. Not even asking the question. She's sitting with us. We walk back to the table. Hollis has already scrounged another seat and everybody scoots down a little. Room for one more at the table. Right next to me.

"Hey guys, this is Kenna Faye. Not sure if you know her, but…" Kenna waves to Bao. He smiles shyly and waves back. Guess they know each other. "Kenna Faye, I see you know Bao. That's Hollis. And next to him is Arthur. Over there is Calvin Sweet and Mike Kot…Sorry Mike."

"Hey, no problem, dere. It's Mikey Kotlowitz. Spelled just like it sounds."

"And next to Mike. Sorry, I don't know your name."

"Oh dis one here." He points to the red-haired girl, who is four to five inches taller than him, seated. Dis one is my little sis, Sarah. Say hello, little sis."

"You're a regular comedian, Mike. Really I'm his big sister. I keep him in line and…"

"Whoa, whoa, whoa. Dat's not what Ma and Dad told me. Dey said I was the older one and you…" Mike's Chicagoland accent is a dead giveaway.

"You wish, Mikey," the girl says. "You wish you were older. And maybe you wish I was your sister too. You perv." She turns to us. "Hi guys. I'm Sarah. Mike's girlfriend."

"Hey now," Mike says. "Don't get started on that 'girlfriend' stuff. Next thing you're gonna want dinners at fancy places…and dancing and diamonds and all dat. Let's just stick with friends."

"If that's the way you want it, Mikey, fine by me."

"Not just friends. We'd still be friends with …what's that thing they say?"

Calvin fills in: "Benefits".

"Yeah dats it. Some of those benefits."

Sarah looks over and shakes her head. "You know, Mike, any time, your Mom is gonna come in and wake you up. Cause you are surely dreaming. Getting yourself all worked up for nothing. Better eat your lunch. Calvin's been staring at your pasta for about ten minutes."

"Have not," says Calvin. "Couldn't eat it if I wanted to. First weigh-in is next week. As captain, I gotta make weight. Set an example for you other guys. Hollis, you gonna make weight?"

Hollis looks up when he hears his name. His face goes red and he bursts into laughter. "Think I'll be OK. I'm just a couple pounds over." Not sure why this is funny, but the whole table explodes in laughter.

"Why are they laughing at you?" I ask. Don't want to be left out of a good joke.

"They're not laughing at me. They're laughing with me. They know I lose eight or ten pounds every practice. Just sweat it out. Heck, I could just skip breakfast and lose five pounds." The table erupts again and Kenna Faye and I join in. I look over at her and smile. She returns it. Calvin and Bao argue about who can go the longest without drinking water. Mike tries to put his arm around Sarah and she elbows him gently in the ribs. She puts her arm around his shoulder instead. Arthur eats one boiled egg and a tiny packet of crackers. Slower than I've ever seen anyone eat in my life.

I turn to Kenna Faye. "Are you OK. Is he…?"

"I'm fine. And he's gone. Left the state."

"Good. That son of a …"

"Let's not talk about it anymore."

"Deal. And don't worry about some guy hurting you…ever again. I've got your back, girlfriend. And I've got a feeling these guys have your back now, too." Nobody at the table paying any attention to us, but in a good way—a nice, inclusive sort of ignoring.

The warning bell for fifth period rings and we all get up. Everybody talks at once. Calvin shoves Mike playfully and Mike pretends to fall down. In slow motion. Sarah grabs his arm and pulls him back up at the last minute.

Push my chair in. Look around the table and smile. I feel…I feel like…I don't know. Something feels like it's changing. Like two of the fifty pounds I carry on my shoulders every day has been lifted. Hollis hands me my backpack, and we all file out, leaving behind the mess of the cafeteria. I give a small wave to the lunch lady, who waits with the other two women to clean up after all of us. She stands stoically, but gives me the smallest nod back.

I actually feel good about going to history

class. Even Mr. Monger's class can't bring me down. I could get used to this.

CHAPTER TWENTY-ONE: HE WHICH HATH NO STOMACH

Most days, getting out of bed is a drag. It's still dark and almost always cold in my room, my little attic hideaway. It wasn't really built to be a bedroom—just a storage space, with no heating ducts. Arvin assures me that heat rises and it will be warm enough all winter. But it's only November and I'm freezing every morning. I need to start sleeping in my hooded sweatshirt. If I have time to wash the stink of the wrestling room out of it before I go to bed. Most nights lately I read Shakespeare sonnets before I fall asleep.

But I digress. While most days have been hard to get out of bed, it's been different the past week or so. Not sure why, but I think lunch has something to do with it. Not that the food I pack has gotten any better. It's pretty much peanut butter and jelly sandwich, ham sandwich, turkey sandwich, bologna sandwich or leftovers. In rotation. The food hasn't gotten better, but the company has.

For the past week, I've become a regular at the wrestling table. That's what I named it and I'm sticking to it. All the regulars are there every day. Calvin, Mike, Bao, Arthur, Hollis and me from the team. A couple of other wrestlers drift in and out, but we're the regulars. Oh, can't forget Kenna Faye and Sarah. They're always there. Kenna Faye was reluctant at first. Didn't feel like she fit in. But the guys have been great with her. If she doesn't want to talk, they don't force it. Let her eat her lunch in peace. But when she gets going on something, she can be pretty hilarious. The other day, she said something so funny it made milk come of Mike's nose. And that pretty much made everyone's day. It takes so little to entertain us.

So this morning it's dark and cold and I hear rain on the roof. But I don't care. I've got my lunch bunch to look forward to. And practice is kind of fun. Hard as hell. Painful sometimes. Embarrassing when I get pounded by Arthur in live wrestling. But kind of interesting and fun anyway.

I throw on the first clean jeans and T-shirt I can find. My shirt is dark blue with Felton Warriors on the front. I used to hate that. Was even embarrassed by the name. But it doesn't bother me anymore. Arthur says if he can handle the stupid name, then I shouldn't let it bother me. So, I'm letting that go.

I'm a little late and it will take longer riding to school in the rain. I grab half a bagel (Walmart's finest) and head for the back door. Geneva says "Bye-bye" and I blow her a kiss. She pretends to catch it and plants it on her cheek. Junior and Denise don't even look up from their cereal. Junior's has turned to mush in the milk because he's messing around again instead of eating. As I reach for the door, June stops me.

"Kayla, when you get home from practice, can you fix supper for everyone?"

"Sure, what's up?"

"I got to take a casserole over to the Richmonds. Pauline is back in the hospital and Ralph is there with all those kids by himself. I'm sure they're not eating anything. Nothin' good anyway. And I got to help him clean up the place.

I'm sure it's a wreck. With Pauline gone and all."

I've never heard her mention the Richmond family before. But OK. "Yeah…I mean yes, ma'am. What should I make?"

"There's Hamburger Helper in the cupboard. Make that noodle one. It's the only one Junior will eat. And make sure that boy eats an apple or somethin' healthy. You hear me, boy?"

Junior's head shoots up from his comics. He wasn't listening, but drones out "Yes ma'am."

"And Kayla, get Geneva washed up and in bed by 8:30. Don't know how long I'll be there."

"Sure." Look at my watch. I need to go. Grab my poncho and I'm off to school. Like Dorothy riding her bike down the road in the movie. Like Dorothy if she moved a couple of states east and started wrestling . What would Auntie Em think of that?

School is…well, school. Four periods, then lunch with friends, then three more. We've all been through it.

After school, I stand in front of my locker sorting my books. I'd like to read more of the Alexie book Arthur gave me, but I have less time with practice every night. Over my right shoulder two shapes slide into my peripheral vision.

"Hey, Kayla. We were hoping to catch you here." It's Donnie, with Todd hanging just behind him.

"What do you want?"

Donnie says, "Why so hostile?" I don't respond and slam my locker door. Turn to face them. Try to walk past, but first Donnie and then Todd block my way. I'm not walking around the long way, so I just stand there and stare.

"Hey," Donnie says, "we've got a friend who wants your number."

"Yeah," Todd chimes in. "He thinks you're hot. He wants to go out with you."

Donnie snickers and repeats, "Yeah, hot."

"Leave me alone." Looking past Todd and Donnie, I see Dave Sperry and Jimmy Dole leaning against a locker about ten feet away. Watching. With amusement. Is it one of them who wants my number? Yuck!

"C'mon, Kayla, don't be that way." Donnie grabs my wrist. I swim out of his grip. Just like Coach taught us on the second day of practice. It works really well. Even in real life.

"Don't touch me, Donnie. Don't ever touch me." Dole looks our way. He's smiling now. Does he think this is funny? Two guys hassling a girl?

"OK, OK. Little miss touchy." Donnie puts up his hands in the 'I'm innocent' pose. "But what do you say? Do you want to meet him? He thinks…" I stop listening because Dole and Sperry are walking this way. Right now. What the hell is going on?

Dole walks up behind Donnie. Puts his hand on his shoulder and turns him around. Todd spins around too. I step to the side, out of the way.

"Has it been a while since you had your hearing checked, Barker? What do you think Dave, does he have a hearing problem?"

Sperry nods and says gravely, "Could be. Could be."

"See, the reason I asked you that is …I don't think you heard the girl right," Jimmy says. "Do you think he heard her, Dave?"

"Must not have," Dave says nonchalantly.

"I don't think so either. But she said for you to leave her alone. Pretty loud and clear. Right

Dave?

"Yeah," Dave says. "I heard it clear enough."

Dave and Jimmy stand toe to toe with Donnie and Todd. Like four gunfighters sizing each other up. Just staring. For five seconds. Then ten.

Finally Jimmy says, "So, why don't you do what the girl says and leave her alone?"

Donnie considers this for a while. Looks at Todd who has nothing to offer. Licks his lips and looks back at Dave and Jimmy.

"Why don't you mind your own business?" Donnie blurts, a little unsure of his word choice.

"Dave, did he just say what I think he said?"

"I believe he said it," says Dave. No emotion whatsoever.

Jimmy turns back to Donnie. "See, if you'd just shut up and walked away, we'd all be good here. But seeing that you didn't, I'm making this my business. Now we, I mean the three of us," Dole motions to include me, "have practice tonight and tomorrow after school. But Saturday would work for me. Should we say eleven in the morning?

Out by the lake? Nobody will bother us out there."

Donnie chokes out, "What are you talking about?"

"The fight. You and me. We're gonna get it on. Mix it up. You know what I'm talkin' about."

Donnie looks over at Todd, who offers nothing. "Oh, sorry Lazby," Jimmy says. "Do you want to get in on it too? Then Dave here can have some fun. Dave, are you free on Saturday?"

Dave smiles and says, "I'll have to check my schedule. But what the heck. Go ahead and pencil me in."

Jimmy turns back to Donnie, whose face is ashen white. He is shaking, just a little. "Unless you have another friend who wants to come along too. Then we can bring Ray in. Do you think Ray could make it Saturday, Dave?" He's clearly enjoying this. It's weird, but kind of fun to watch.

"Oh, you know Ray. He's always up for an ass kicking"

"Well, great then. It's a plan. Heck, you guys ought to go ahead and pack a lunch. We'll probably be out there a while. You may need a little snack. Between rounds. Will that work for your guys?"

Donnie's mouth moves but he says nothing. Looks at Todd, then looks down at the ground. I'd pay ten bucks to be inside his head right now. Finally, Donnie has something to say. "I got to go. I'm late for…" Doesn't finish his sentence. Slides between Dave, Jimmy and me and takes off down the hallway.

Jimmy looks over at Todd, who seems to be frozen. "What about you, Lazby?"

Todd Lazby finally finds his voice. "What?" It's all he can come up with.

"Are you late too?" Todd says nothing, but sees his opportunity. Follows in Donnie's path. Quite a bit faster though.

"I thought that went well. What do you think, Dave?" Jimmy quips. How did this guy get so glib?

Dave nods his head. "About like normal." They both turn and look at me. Like they are waiting for me to jump in.

I do. "Are you guys crazy? Getting into a fight with those idiots? You know you'd get kicked off the team and…"

"Kayla, Kayla, Kayla. There wasn't a fight. Wasn't ever going to be a fight."

Now it's my turn to play dumb. Or actually be dumb. "What do you…"

Jimmy cuts me off "There wasn't going to be a fight because punks like those two never fight. They're all talk. No action. Right Dave?"

"No action," Dave repeats.

Jimmy looks at me seriously. "Besides, if anybody was going to kick their ass, it would have been you. So we just saved *you* from getting booted off the team."

I laugh a little and they both join in. Who would have thought I'd be having this conversation? With these guys.

Jimmy looks at his watch and motions to Dave. Dave nods and they both turn to leave. Take two steps and then Jimmy Dole grabs Sperry's arm. Turns him around to face me. "Hey Dave, how much would you have paid to see Kayla ram that little punk into the trophy case?"

Dave smiles and his face lights up. He thinks for a second and says, "Jimmy, I would have paid any amount of money I could get my hands on to see that."

"Me too, Dave. Me too."

They turn and walk away without saying a word. Get halfway down the hall and Jimmy turns around again. "Hey Kayla. Bring your little boyfriend down to wrestle on our end of the mat sometime. We won't bite. Will we, Dave?"

Dave smiles again and shakes his head no. "At least not while Coach is looking."

They laugh together and walk away. I grab my backpack. Walk toward the back door. Smiling the whole way. Life is full of surprises. My life, anyway.

CHAPTER TWENTY-TWO: THEY BURN UP IN VICTORY

Saturday afternoon before my first match on Tuesday and Arvin is off working on the wrestling room. Wrestling barn. Whatever. I thought farmers just took it easy all winter, but that guy works just as hard in the winter as summertime. Maybe harder. June is pulling an extra shift at the bakery today. She missed a day last week for the Richmond lady's funeral. Denise is at a friend's house, and Geneva is playing with her cousins in St. Luke. It's just Junior and me at the kitchen table. I'm supposed to watch him, but the kid ignores about ninety percent of what I say. So I just make sure he doesn't burn the house down or something stupid like that.

I do my history homework while he reads the newspaper. Something in the paper makes him laugh hysterically. Non-stop for about two minutes. I'm sure he's faking it. Then I can't take anymore.

"Junior, are the comics really that funny?"

"I'm not reading the comics," he says. "They don't have comics in the Sheffield paper, dope." Just when I think he can't come up with another way to insult me, he pulls out something new. He pushes the paper toward me, covering the sheet I'm writing on.

"Check this out," says Junior. "It can't be real." I glance at the headline. "Car Rolls Down Spring Hill; Crashes into House Below".

"I don't think that's very funny, Junior. Somebody could have gotten hurt when that car…" He cuts me off.

"Not that one. Duh! The one about the dog."

Above the headline is a series of three pictures, with the caption: "Think Dogs Can't Climb Trees? Kelly Shows They Can!"

"Why is that so funny?" I ask.

"It's gotta be fake. Nobody could ever teach a dog to climb trees. Could they?" First time he's ever asked me a serious question.

"I don't know. I guess it's real. They've got the pictures and everything. I don't think a reporter would lie about what he saw." Junior grabs the paper back and studies the picture. Not laughing now. He's clearly fascinated with the tree-climbing dog.

He's serious now. "Would you take me to see it sometime?"

"What? That dog?"

"Yeah. That would be really cool. Would you?"

"Junior, I can't drive. I don't have a license. Or a car."

"Just get your boyfriend to take us."

"What boyfriend?"

"Hollis. I saw him drop you off the other night. Did you guys kiss?" He makes a series of annoying kissing sounds and then starts a new round of laughter.

"Hollis is not my boyfriend. He's my…" What is he? "He's just a friend. And my wrestling teammate."

"But you could still get him to take us to town to see this dog. Would you, Kayla? Please." He smiles as he says 'Please'. Seems genuine. Looks like a normal little boy when he's not trying to be some evil twit.

"I'll ask him sometime. But we won't have time until the season's over. And it just gets started next week."

"Can I come to see you wrestle?" Junior asks.

"Not the first match. I don't want anybody…"

"You don't want anybody to see you get creamed by a boy?"

"No, I just…" Actually he's right. "OK, I don't want anybody to see me get creamed by a boy. Maybe another match. After I know whether I can do this."

"OK. That would be cool. Don't you want to see this dog climb a tree, too?" Actually, I do. "Yeah, I guess that would be pretty OK." He nods his head and goes back to his reading. See Junior, we can get along if you just make the smallest effort. Denise, though, is another story.

Tuesday. 5 pm. In the locker room at Garner. The visitors' locker room. The team's all dressed. I join them after changing in the girls' room down the hall. Some lady came in and saw me in my uniform. My singlet. She just stared without saying a word. With the team huddled around them, Calvin and Stefano give us a pep talk before the meet. My team. Our team.

"OK, guys, first match of the season." Calvin gets us started. "We need a total team effort. With Jimmy out, we're down six points before we start. We need everybody else to step up."

Stefano joins in. "Let's get coach his first win tonight. Then the pressure's off." Murmurs of assent all around.

"Right," says Calvin. "Our schedule is just gonna get harder toward the end. So this is one we can pick off right away."

"For you new guys, when we go out there for warmups, they'll be on their sidelines. Watching us," Stefano warns. "Don't even glance in their direction. Act like they don't exist. Pretend this is our house. Because tonight, it is."

Calvin finishes it off. "OK, let's break it down on Kayla." They've never done this before. I get into the referee's position—hands and knees—and feel a bunch of hands on my back. It's weird. Like I can feel their support, through their hands. I'm ready.

"OK, Felton Pride on three," I shout. "One, two, three!"

Twelve voices respond. "Felton Pride!"

Calvin leads the way and we charge out the door. Head for the mat and begin our jog around it. A smattering of boos from the crowd, but they are mostly silent. A couple of guys throw their headgear toward our seating area, so I do the same thing. As we round their side of the mat, I see their team out of the corner of my eye. Like Stefano said, they are staring at us. When we run past the fans the third time, I distinctly hear the word "girl." Next time around I hear it three times and somebody points. The following time, there is a general buzz in the stands. They are all talking about me. Crap. I'm not ready for this. I don't know anything about wrestling. I…

Arthur grabs my arm and pulls me to the center of the mat. We begin drilling. First takedowns, then escapes, then reversals. A couple of breakdowns. I break a little sweat. No longer thinking about the crowd. At the end of drilling, we form a tight circle in the center of the mat. Our heads all point inward. Nobody says anything for a minute, then Calvin looks in my direction.

"Kayla's up first," Calvin says. "OK guys, let's send her off right." In order, starting with Calvin, they go around the circle and gently slap the top of my hand with theirs. At the end, Stefano raises his hand a few inches off the mat and everyone follows. I'm a little slow, but I pick up the ritual. He nods his head and we all slap the mat in unison. Then we're up and headed for our chairs. On the opposite side from the Garner team.

The referee strides out, signals to both benches and says, "Captains?" Stefano and Calvin walk back to the center of the mat and shake hands with the Garner team captains. One smaller guy and two big guys. Coach grabs my arm. Pulls me out of my seat and takes me behind the rest of the guys.

"OK, Kayla, you're up first. Just be relaxed out there and use what you've learned. Nothing fancy. Just stick to basics. You ready?"

I try to answer, but my head is spinning. I think about the scene near the end of the Harry Potter series, when Harry goes into an all-white room. At first he sees nothing, then a few things come into focus. I feel like my vision is constricting. Am I going to pass out? The referee looks to our bench and asks "106?"

I run out to the mat and take my place on the starting line. Where's the other guy? The referee walks over, leans in toward me and says quietly, "First match?" I nod. "Check in at the scorer's table." I look around. He points to the side of the room. "Over there." I give them my name and then run back out to the mat. I've never been more scared in my life. Look up in time to see the other guy walk in. A little kid. Looks like he's maybe 12 or 13. But he has to be in high school. Doesn't he? He looks up with a panicked expression. This kid is just as scared as I am! This won't be …

"Shake hands," says the ref and I step forward and give the kid my strongest grip. He looks down at our hands, joined there in the center. We step back to our lines and immediately the whistle blows. Move to my right and circle, then circle again. Keep a good stance. Hands out in blocking position. Guard my legs. When is something going to happen?

"Head work, Kayla!" shouts Coach P.

I reach for the boy's head and pull it down. He resists and turns slightly to his right. My left. I see his reaction and reach for his head again. His head snaps back and he turns to my left again. Action and reaction. I shoot for his left leg. Got it. Lift it off the ground. To my waist, then chest high. He's hopping, but not going down. What do I…?

As if reading my mind, Coach shouts, "Trip. Trip him!" Sweep his leg out with my right one and he's down. I'm on top of him fast and hear the ref signal "two" for a takedown. That was easy. Now what? The kid squirms up from the mat. I use my hand around his waist to drive him down, but he's back up again. He lunges forward and the whistle blows. We're out of bounds.

Coach P claps encouragement. "Kayla, break him down and go to work."

Ref restarts the match, and I reach for the boy's right ankle. Pull up his ankle while forcing him down to the mat on his left side. He breaks down flat on the mat, then reaches back for my head with his left hand. We've drilled what to do in this situation in practice. But I can't remember. From the sideline, my teammates scream in unison "Half!

Half him! Do it, now!"

Bring my left arm up and over his head. Start pushing with all my might. Harder now and...he turns to his back. I keep the half nelson in and get into the chest-to-chest position. The kid is in trouble. Panicked. He squirms up once, then back to his shoulders. Twice, back to his shoulders and stays down. The ref is on the mat—right beside us. Studies the boy's back for a couple of seconds and slaps the mat. A cheer goes up from our sideline. Is that it? That ended so fast. I help the boy up. Shake hands with him. The ref raises my hand, and I run back to our sideline.

High fives, back slaps, "Nice match" and "Way to go" all down the line. I grab a water bottle from our cooler and take a long sip. Walk back along our sideline and take a seat alongside Emmy, Coach Pettus' son. He smiles and shakes my hand.

"Good job out there, Kayla. You look like an old pro."

"I've got a good teacher," I explain.

"Yeah, the old man knows a couple things about wrestling."

"You wouldn't be calling him 'old man' if

you practiced with us. You'd be running laps all practice."

Emmy laughs and we follow Arthur's progress on the mat. He's got one of their team captains. A very tough match, but Arthur wins 6-4. Stefano pins his guy in a hurry and we're ahead 15-0. Bao and Emmy both win close matches, putting us ahead 21-0. We may get the win coach needs in our first match. My lunch pal, Mike, gets pinned in the first period, and they cut our lead to 21-6. Calvin wins at 145 pounds to put us up 24-6. Looking good.

Then the wheels fall off our little engine that could. We lose 152 and 160 pound matches by pin, and we're only up by six. I'm shocked that Ray Harding and Dave Sperry both lose. They seem distracted and Coach shouts little, if any advice during their matches. Just lets them wrestle. Both lose their matches on points, and we're down by nine. Jimmy Dole is not here for some reason and Garner takes a forfeit at 195. Down 12 now. We can't win. Ernesto draws their other team captain at 220 pounds. He holds on until the end, but gets pinned with just 10 seconds remaining. Just Hollis' match left. He's much bigger than the boy he's wrestling and about six inches taller. Is that fair? I guess anything goes at Heavyweight. Just like my opponent, the kid looks terrified. Hollis works in close to his opponent. His arms inside the other guy's arms and around his lower rib cage. Pulls the guy in, turns his hip to the right and throws the boy. Straight to his back, with Hollis on top. Ref gets into position fast and calls the pin. In just 22 seconds! Great match. But the scoreboard says it all. Pirates 45 - Visitors 33. If we just had Jimmy. Where is he?

I walk into the kitchen back home. June does the dishes while Arvin sips his coffee from a gray Gray's Bakery mug, flipping through the morning paper that he never gets to read in the morning. In the background, the Sheffield radio station plays quietly. A guy sings a country song about his daughter asking him not to walk so fast. A sad song about a sad family. Arvin puts down his paper and says, "Hey there, girl."

June turns and wipes her hands on her apron. Sets the pot she was drying back on the stove, blows a stray hair out of her eye and looks my way. "Well, you made it home safe. No broken bones or nothing?"

I smile and say nothing. Can't get this stupid grin off my face.

"Well," June says, "don't just stand there grinnin' like a possum. How'd you do?"

"I won!" I blurt out, way too excited for just one win. "Pinned the guy in the first period."

"Well, how de do about that?" Arvin says, looking astonished.

June says, "Well, huh," and starts for the fridge. "You ready for some supper?" I nod yes. A shower can wait. Throw my gym bag in the corner and sit down next to Arvin. When June turns to get the food, Arvin pats my hand and winks. They can be alright. Sometimes. In their own way.

CHAPTER TWENTY-THREE: TO MAKE A MAN
LOOK SAD

Before the couple of classes that I share with Madison and Raven start, I generally try to ignore their drivel. They seem to have the intellectual curiosity of cacti, and they can be so damn mean. For no good reason at all. Mean to random kids, mean to their groupies and mean to each other. I'll never understand the pleasure they seem to get in making a high school kid feel worse about herself than she already does. I mean, we're all stuck in these hell holes, right? Except for the kids whose parents let them drop out at sixteen. But I feel more sorry for them than anyone. Sure they are done with school. But I can't imagine the life they face. But today, for whatever reason, Madison and Raven play nice. At least with each other.

Madison says, "Your hair looks really cute today. Did you get it done at the Stylette?"

"No," Raven replies. "Mom took us up to the city on Saturday. Went to Curl Up and Dye. Then we hung out at Castleton. Saw some hotties at the food court."

"Well, thanks for inviting me."

"She just took me and the bratty twins."

"Your nails are cute too," Madison says, "What is that?"

"It's called Petal to the Metal. Get it?" Raven flashes her nails for anybody interested to see. Few notice. "Because of the flower petals? Isn't that the cutest? It was between that and Tenacious Teal. But that's so…"

"Right, like so totally last week and…"

Mr. Chenoweth clears his throat and the chatter dies down. Except for Madison and Raven, who can be heard giggling over some no-doubt scathingly brilliant witticism. Love when I can work Haley Mills' "scathingly brilliant" into a thought. Even if nobody else hears it.

Chenoweth intercedes. "Girls, quiet down. It's time to get started and we…"

First period announcements come on the intercom. Usually, they are a real snooze fest. Tons of information on stuff I couldn't care less about. But midway through the spiel, the vice principal announces the sports scores.

"The girls volleyball team won in three sets to two over Southwestern on Friday. The boys basketball team lost 63-59 to Morristown Saturday night. And in the first meet of the season, the Felton wrestling club lost 45-33 to Garner on Tuesday. Winning their first matches for the team were Kayla Burbadge at 106 pounds and Hollis Fleming at 285. So be sure to congratulate these students who…"

They move in unison. Just like the beginning of school, twenty-eight sets of eyes turn in my direction. And this time…I don't care. Don't even care that they just announced to the whole school how much I weigh. I just stare ahead. No smile, no glare. Just my everyday face.

Mr. C breaks the trance my presence seems to have put everyone into. "Well, that is great news. I'm sure that the whole class would like to congratulate Kayla on her win."

And I'm just as sure that they don't want to do that. Nobody offers so much as a smile, nod or thumbs-up in my direction. Most people have turned around and forgotten me. But Raven and Madison can't seem to look away. Their faces reflecting something bordering on shock. That anyone would mention me at this school. For any reason. Raven shakes her head and I see Madison mouth "I know."

Chenoweth continues. "As I mentioned a couple of days ago, we're going to work in pairs to write our sonnets. You don't have to work alone like the Bard did. That's a nickname for Shakespeare. I'm just going to assign the pairs alphabetically." He picks up his grade book. "Jim Allison, you'll work with Charlotte Atwood. Madison Bell, you and Kayla Burbadge will be partners. Gina…"

Madison's hand is up in a flash. "Mr. Chenoweth, can Raven and I work together? We've been talking about it and we want…"

"No. For this assignment, I want people to work with their assigned partners. You may get to know something about somebody you don't know so well."

Madison has stopped listening. She looks at

Raven for support, her mouth open like one of those clowns in a carnival game. Her face drops, and she looks like she's going to cry. Seriously, what a drama queen. Am I really that hideous to her? Anyway, not my problem. I can write a sonnet in my sleep, so she won't hold me back any. And maybe…

In the hall after class Mike and Sarah walk toward me. Sarah's red hair looks like a crown as she towers over Mike. About five feet before reaching me, Mike starts a chant. "Who da man? Kayla da man! Who da man? Kayla da man!" Several kids turn to see who Mike's yelling about. As I pass by, he offers his palm with the customary, "Don't leave me hangin'." We slap hands and I walk on.

Walking behind Mike, a boy from my math class says, "Great job, Kayla!" and a couple of kids look in my direction. Someone on the other side of the hall points toward me. I'm shocked that the boy would know my name. We've never spoken before. I mumble "Thanks," and keep walking to music class.

At practice that night, I ask Arthur the

question that was burning in my mind at the wrestling match. At the time, I forgot to ask anyone because I was basically as scared as I've ever been. Followed by being pretty darn elated. So now's my chance.

"Hey partner."

"Hi Kayla." He's reading again. Just holds up the book so I can check it out. He's getting to know me. It's something about grass. By Susan Powers. That much I can make out.

"I was wondering."

"Inquiring minds do want to know."

"Funny. But really. Why do our uniforms say 'PAL' on them? Does it stand for something?"

"Yep," Arthur quips.

"What does it stand for?"

"Police Athletic League."

"And what, pray tell, is a Police Athletic League?"

"As long as you're praying, I'm telling."

"Please do. Inquiring minds and all that."

"The PAL is in Indianapolis. A wrestling club run by the police department there. Mostly for troubled kids. Some in gangs and broken homes and stuff. Coach volunteered there when he first moved to Indiana. When we started having matches at Felton, they donated their old uniforms to us and got some new ones."

"Oh, that's cool. And kind of funny."

"Why funny?"

"Because it will mess with the heads of every team we wrestle. Trying to figure out what it means. We should never tell them. Or make up some huge lie. Anything to distract them."

"I like the way you think. It's devious and twisted, but I like it. But you're likely to be a bigger distraction to teams than any uniform."

I hope that's not the case. The whistle blows and we're jogging. Still can't get Arthur to wrestle over near Dave Sperry and Jimmy Dole. Practice is practice. It's not the same every day, but it's hard and sweaty and stinky. And tiring. Really tiring. When Coach signals a five-minute break, I head outside to the Portajohn. Two figures lurk in the shadow beside the barn. There are noises like coughing and sniffing. A couple of words, then quiet. Out of the dark, Dave Sperry approaches me.

"Stay away from him," Dave orders.

"Stay away from who?" I ask

"Jimmy. Just leave him alone. He's…"

Then I hear it distinctly. A sob, coming from the lone figured slumped on the ground just past Sperry. I walk over. But Sperry takes my arm, gently. I look down at it and he immediately releases me. I walk over to see Jimmy crying quietly. He doesn't know I'm there. Reaching down, I gently touch his back. His head jerks back. His face rains tears and snot drips from both nostrils. Like a fountain.

Red faced and angry he hisses, "Don't…touch me."

I wait a few seconds then put my arm around his shoulder. At first he tries to jerk away, but I hold tight. He doesn't fight my grip. Just stares at the ground and sobs.

"Jimmy, what's wrong?"

He says nothing. Just the tears.

"What happened?" I ask "Did somebody hurt you?"

He shakes his head and looks up. His cheeks are red and blotched. "She's…she's gone."

"Who is gone?"

"Mother Richmond."

I remember. The funeral last week. The one June took off work for.

"Who is Mother Richmond? I mean, who is she to you?"

"She's...she was my foster mom. The only one...who...who..."

I ask, "The only one who what, Jimmy?"

"The only person who really cared about me. In my whole crappy life. And now she's ...she's..." He can't finish. Buries his head in his hands and racking sobs erupt from him.

I start again. "Jimmy. Jimmy, listen to me."

"What?"

"This won't mean anything to you now, but I'm gonna tell you anyway. This hurt. This pain you're feeling now. I know it's awful. You feel like you want to die. But things will get better. I know and..."

"You don't know crap," Jimmy says. "Nothing about me. My life. You had a Mom and a Dad who loved you. And now you got a family here. I've never had nothing or nobody. My whole life. Till Mother Richmond and she's..."

Arthur sticks his head out the barn door and shouts. "Kayla! Kayla?"

"I'm over here. Be in in a minute. Tell Coach there was a line for the john." Arthur shrugs. Sperry walks back into practice beside him. The barn door closes behind them. I stay kneeling by Jimmy's side.

"Jimmy, I need to get back into practice. If you ever want to talk about this….I can ..I'm…"

"OK," he sniffles and slumps down with a deep sigh. I give his shoulder a final squeeze and rise. Walk to the door.

"Kayla." I turn. Jimmy remains kneeling in the shadows. "Don't say anything. In there. About this." I shake my head no. Open the door and look into the light in the barn.

A small voice in the dark says softly, "And thanks."

The team has already started drilling. Arthur and Dave stand next to each other, jogging in place. Arthur looks at me with a puzzled expression and I shake my head. He and I start to drill and Coach walks over.

"Where's Dole?" Dave shrugs and Coach

looks at me. He better not be outside smoking again or I'll..."

"Coach? Mr. Pettus?" I stammer. Dave shoots me a warning glance. "Jimmy is outside. He got poked in the eye pretty good working out. He's washing it out." Dave looks over at me. His eyes widen.

After ten minutes, Jimmy rejoins the practice and begins drilling with Dave. Arthur and I continue our workout as he enters, still at the opposite end of the mat. Another forty-five minutes and we're through. Coach gives a brief intro to our meet next week at Edinboro High. Then we are free to go. Out into the world. The big wide non-wrestling world out there. I collect my gear and make my way out.

"Hey, Kayla." It's Arthur. I turn and he walks to my side. "You're starting to get it now."

"I've still got a long way to go in wrestling and I..."

"I'm not talking about wrestling."

I think about this for a minute and nod. "Maybe we're both getting it. And can we move our workout to the other end tomorrow? There's plenty of room down there."

Arthur doesn't respond, but turns to gaze at the far end of the mat. Dave and Jimmy both kneel and look down. Coach kneels between them, his large arms around both boys' shoulders. Coach says something quietly and then looks at Jimmy for a long time. Jimmy nods.

I open the front door of the barn and walk into the cold Indiana night. But I don't feel the chill as I crunch over the gravel toward my bike. It's gone. Already in the back of Hollis' truck with the passenger side door open. Heat blasting and a song by a famous local guy playing on the radio. I climb in without a word.

CHAPTER TWENTY-FOUR: BETWEEN THE DRAGON AND HIS WRATH

Time passes. Here in Felton, just like in Chicago. I guess you don't have to be a physicist to figure that out, but it seemed a while ago like the clock and calendar got stuck. Right around April 20. Then, as if somebody changed a watch battery or ripped a few pages out of a calendar, time started moving again. Not sure exactly when, but I definitely feel it now.

And I've got a somewhat predictable schedule. Wake up, get dressed, down my ladder, make my own breakfast, avoid any of Junior's pranks, ignore Denise's general meanness, feed the dogs, then off to school. Unless it's snowing, I still ride my bike every day. Hollis has given me a lift a few times. But lately, so have Calvin and Bao and Mike and a couple of the other guys. I was truly shocked last week when Jimmy and Dave pulled up and offered me a ride. Mostly shocked because it meant they were showing up for first period on time. Miracles can and do happen.

Then it's four periods (snore) and lunch with my friends (yay). Then three more classes and final bell. Grab my bike, pedal the half mile to the barn and practice from 4-6. Home for dinner (or supper, if you prefer), feed the dogs again and I have a couple of hours for homework. Or whatever. I know, it doesn't sound like much, but it's a life. My life at least. And I'm happy just watching most days roll by.

The wrestling season is…well, pretty sad so far. We are 0-6, with an uphill battle the rest of the way. Most of the easy teams are behind us. We had our best chance to beat Garner, but we blew it. If only Jimmy had been there. Oh. My. God. I can't believe I would think such a thing. Poor guy. It's not his fault. Any of it.

My record is a little better. I'm 4-2 right now. Two regular wins and two forfeits. Nobody told me that 106 pounders get quite a few forfeits. It's kind of weird to walk out there and have them declare me the winner for doing nothing. Just for being there, I guess. My two losses were not awful. One of them was 5-3. In the other, I got pinned, but not till the third period. Coach has warned us all about post-match conduct. Be a good sport—win or lose. Don't gloat about wins. No fist pumping or anything. And no sulking about losses. If you give 100% and lose, so be it. Shake the guy's hand, walk off the mat and learn from whatever mistakes you made. You'll get to wrestle another day.

We wrestle tonight at Kingsport. Each school has a different system for weighing me in. Some do it with a female coach, some with a teacher. I even had a wrestler's mom weigh me in before. Most have been pretty nice. Some tell me that I'm brave and they could never do what I do. But the woman who weighs me in tonight clearly doesn't like me. Says nothing. Just gives me her best stink eye. Step on the scale and I'm a pound under. She just nods, make a note on her sheet and walks off in huff. Wow, who peed in her Cheerios? It sure wasn't me.

When we do warm-ups, I notice the same woman standing near the visitor's bench. She talks to the opposing coach, actually talking at him, gesturing toward our bench, then over at their wrestlers. Then back at us again. Exchanges a few words with the coach. Apparently doesn't like what she hears and stomps off, walks into the stands and sits down—glaring at us. We finish our warm-ups, do our rituals and take our seats.

I've got my head gear on and I'm ready to go. Getting loose on my own, while Calvin and Stefano meet the other captains. Coach has told me to walk out of sight while getting ready for my match. Resist the temptation to look at my opponent. "It doesn't matter who he is," Coach has said at least two dozen times to the team. "He's a guy who's come to wrestle. Treat him with respect, but don't fear him. Expect to win every match. It's why we train so hard every day. It's why we step on the mat. To win." The ref calls "106" to both benches. I check in at the scorer's table and run out to the mat and take my starting position on my starting line. And wait. And wait. Ref looks over at the Kingsport bench and says "106?" again. The coach crosses his arms and shakes his head. The ref comes back to the center and takes my arm. "Forfeit," he says, and raises my arm above my head.

A smattering of boos from the crowd. It

grows until it rises into a loud chorus. I steal a glance into their stands and standing up, egging the opposing fans on, is the woman who weighed me in. I trot back to the bench and Coach is shaking his head. He gently takes me by the shoulder and leads me to a seat on the end, next to him. "Just ignore them, Kayla. Act like you can't hear it."

I'm the daughter of an actor. I can fake it real good. But I can hear them.

So after my forfeit win, things started going downhill—fast . First Arthur, then Stefano, then Bao lost. We didn't get a win until Don Montgomery won at 152. I felt good for Don, because it was his first win of the year. The guys gave him a lot of props. Even the guys who had already lost gave him high fives. In the end, the score was not pretty. Kingsport 45 - Felton 18. We are 0-7, with just six matches to go. Not promising.

After Hollis' match, Calvin prompts us to line up. He and Stefano go first and the first of us fall in line behind our fearless leaders. When I've shaken the last guy's hand, I turn to head back to our bench. Somebody grabs my arm and spins me around. The coach for the other team. He pulls me three feet away and starts shouting. Loud. In my face. Is this really happening?

"What do you think you're doing?" he yells. "Goin' out there and takin' a win away from one of our top guys. You don't belong out there and I…"

Footsteps behind me on the mat. Coming up fast. You don't normally hear guys walk on the mat because when the soft wrestling shoes meet the soft mat, there's almost no sound. Not like the squeaks you hear on a basketball court. But I can hear these steps loud and clear. Uneven. Like tap, pop, tap, pop. Coach Pettus forces himself between the other coach and me. Doesn't touch me, but moves the other coach back about three feet. Fast, with his upper body. I should leave, but I just stand behind them. Too numb to move. The other coach starts to speak, but Coach Pettus cuts him off, immediately.

"Don't you ever put your hands on one of my wrestlers again. You hear me, Ron?" Everybody in the whole gym hears him.

"You know as well as me that no girl belongs on that mat," the Kingsport coach says. "She cost my guy a win and he's got college scouts here tonight and …"

"I know this much. I put a wrestler out there. Somebody ready to wrestle. She didn't cost anybody anything. Somebody else cost him a loss. I don't care who. And don't think he would have gotten a win anyway. You want to go an exhibition match right now?"

"He ain't wrestling no girl. It ain't right."

"OK, he won't wrestle and she won. Fair and square. End of conversation. Unless you want to discuss this further. Outside." Coach Pettus spits the last words at him and glares. I've seen him mad a couple of times in practice. When one of the guys is goofing off. But never like this. He's in the guy's face, which is crimson, by the way. The other coach starts to sputter something. Thinks better of it. Turns and walks away. Coach lets out a long breath and shakes his head. Turns back toward me and walks. I turn and join him walking when he reaches me.

In a low voice, he says, "Sorry you had to hear that, Kayla. He's wrong. Don't take it personally and just…"

Don't hear any more of what he says. I'm shaking so hard I can barely walk. A swirl of emotions engulfs me. I feel guilty and sad and angry and afraid. All at the same time.

    This is not a good night. The ride home in Hollis' truck seems to take forever. The country roads we roll down are dark and cold. I cry myself to sleep in the passenger seat.

CHAPTER TWENTY-FIVE: FOR THY SWEET LOVE REMEMBERED

I wake up with a start. What a weird dream. About the Felton Walker. There's a guy here who walks all over town. All day, every day. Not sure what his name is. Not sure why he does so much walking. I just know what people call him. In my dream, I was walking out of Felton. Headed north. Away from our house. The Felton Walker meets me at the edge of town. He blocks my way. I try to walk around him but he keeps moving in front of me. He's not mad or anything. He's smiling. Seems like a nice man. I ask him politely if I can get by and he shakes his head no. I ask him why and he still doesn't say anything. Then he points back into the town. I don't understand, but he continues to point and smile. I ask him, "Do you want me to turn around?" He nods. I turn around and there are people, lots of people behind me. They all urge me to join them. I start walking in their direction and suddenly, I wake up.

Look at my clock. Damn! It's 10:30. Did I not set my alarm last night? And why didn't June or somebody else wake me up? Jump out of bed. Dress in clothes from the floor, hustle down my ladder and sprint to the kitchen. It's deserted. Of course it is. A note sits in the middle of the empty kitchen table. I grab it and read silently.

Hey girl, You was a wreck last night. Looked all wore out and a little sick. I called the school and said you'd be in late today. That you needed to stay in bed for a while. You need to get more sleep if you're gonna keep up this wrestling thing. Get to bed earlier. So just get over to school when you can. Let the office know when you come in. - June

P.S. Denise is gonna meet you at practice. Emerson said it's OK if she watches. I don't want her riding home alone after dark. So see that she gets home safe with you.

If I'm gonna keep up this wrestling thing. That's a big if. When I get to school, I check the janitor's closet. It's locked. Coach always keeps it open during the day. Where is he? I can't go searching the halls, so I head to the school office. To let them know I'm here. Then join my previously scheduled class, already in progress.

At practice after school, I see Denise's bike outside the barn. She sits on the side of the mat, by herself, doing her homework. Doesn't look up when I approach her or say "hi." Fine. Be that way. I don't have anything to say to you anyway.

When Coach walks into the wrestling room, he blows his whistle right away to start practice. I catch him at the edge of the mat.

"Mr. Pettus?" I correct myself. "Coach? Can I talk to you before practice? It's important." He looks me over. I haven't changed into my workout gear and I still wear my sneakers. He motions me to the corner of the room.

"Stefano and Calvin," Coach P says. "Do your warm-ups and then get practice going. Start drilling takedowns. Your choice. Practice your three best moves."

I'm already in the corner, dreading this. He walks over with a serious expression.

"What's going on Kayla?"

Where to start? "It's about last night. I'm

not sure I should wrestle any more. I don't want to cause trouble everywhere we go. I don't want to be a distraction. Maybe it would be best if…"

He stops me. Knows where this is going. He sighs and looks me in the face. Serious expression. I've really made him mad.

"Kayla. About last night. That guy was wrong. That whole crowd was wrong. They are just a bunch of soreheads who got stirred up by the coach and that boy's mom. I've seen her in action before. She's a piece of work."

The woman who weighed me in. How did I not realize that?

"Kayla, I want you to stay on this team. Your teammates need you. And you need us too, Kayla. It's a two-way street."

"But I was so scared last night. And confused. I felt sick. I don't want to feel that way anymore."

"I can't guarantee you that it won't happen again. In fact, I'm pretty sure that it will. Not in the same way, maybe. But it'll probably happen. And you can handle it, because you handled the situation perfectly last night. Didn't argue or fight or yell. Just stood your ground like a strong young woman. Like a wrestler. One I'm proud to have on my team."

"I just don't want to be the bad guy."

"Bad guy?" Pettus laughs. "You were pretty darn far from being the bad guy last night. Somebody else was the bad guy. You only did what you were supposed to. You took the mat like any other wrestler."

"But what if there are others? Like that guy?"

"Kayla, I want you to listen to me. You did nothing wrong. According to IHSAA rules, girls are allowed to wrestle on high school wrestling teams. Against boys or against girls, if you ever face one. But here's the important thing." He pauses and takes a long drink from his water bottle. "Your whole life you're gonna run into people who will want to tell you what you can't do. Where you can't go. Try to put limits on you. Hold you back."

"I guess so, but…"

"There's no 'but'. They *will* do that. I speak from experience. Do you understand what I mean?"

I do understand, so I nod my head and wait.

He continues, "What I'm talking about here is a life lesson. Not just about a wrestling match. You may not realize it, but you've got a long, long life ahead. If I'm any judge of character, you're gonna have a good life. No, probably a great life. But you've got to make an important decision right now."

"What decision?"

"Are you going to let small-minded people, like that coach and that boy's mom, make your decisions for you? You've shown a hell of lot of courage already. In joining the team. Struggling through practices. Wrestling in matches. People who've never wrestled don't realize the terror involved in stepping on that mat for the first time." He pauses a couple of seconds and puts his hand on my shoulder. "And what you did for Jimmy."

He knows about that? How?

"So now, you've got to decide if you want to continue to show your courage. If so, you can get changed and join the team for practice. But no thinking about it this time. I want you to decide now."

I came into the barn with my mind made up. But maybe Coach is right. I think back to an incident in Chicago when a group of drunk Cubs fans were hassling a homeless guy in Uptown one afternoon. My mom stood up to them. Told them they should be ashamed of themselves. Stood there staring them down till they laughed and left. Then she gave the homeless guy twenty bucks and walked him down to the Salvation Army food truck. I remember how proud of her I was that day. Proud of the brave thing she did. Proud that she was my mom. I'd like for my daughter to think of me that way someday.

"Well?" Coach looks at me with a questioning expression.

"OK."

"OK, what?" He's going to make me say it.

"I'll stay with the team."

"Good decision. And I can promise you this. Write this down if you want to. Some day in the future, you'll think back to this day and remember. And you'll be really glad that you stuck it out here. Give me a call when that day happens. You can call me collect."

I laugh. "I don't even know what calling collect means."

He shakes his head and laughs. "Now I feel like an old man."

"You didn't look like an old man last night. You moved across that mat pretty fast!"

He laughs again and offers his large hand. I put out my little hand and we shake.

"Now get changed and get on the mat. You're late, so you've got to work extra hard today."

After practice, a few of the guys huddle together. As I walk over toward Denise, Arthur yells my name and motions me over.

"The guys are planning a party in a couple of weeks," Arthur says, enthusiastically.

"And this won't be any old party," Arthur explains. "We're planning a wrestling pitch-in!"

"OK, I'll bite. What's a wrestling pitch-in? Inquiring minds want to know."

"A wrestling pitch-in is when a bunch of wrestlers get together. Everybody brings their favorite candy bars, donuts, brownies, Twinkies, cupcakes and stuff. Everything you've been craving if you're cutting weight. Put it all on a big blanket and mix it up. Then everybody takes whatever they want."

Bao smiles. "I hope somebody brings some Gray's brownies. Somebody. Somebody." Bao looks at me and all of the guys laugh.

"But if you eat all of that candy and junk, won't you guys be over weight?" I ask.

"Not a problem," Calvin grins. "We only plan a wrestling pitch-in when we have a long break between matches. After the party, no more matches for nine days. We can all get back down by then. But for this one night. Sweetness!"

Hollis asks, "So, Kayla, can you come?"

"I don't know. It sounds like a guy thing."

Bao says seriously, "You are one of the guys, Kayla."

I hesitate and there is a chorus of "C'mon" and "It'll be fun".

"Alright, I'll talk to my parents about it. I mean June and Arvin." Forgot that Denise is waiting. She's being really patient. "I gotta get Denise home." We say our goodbyes and I walk to edge of the mat where Denise sits reading. My book. *Shakespeare's Sonnets.*

"Hi Denise."

"Hi," she says. Wow, that's progress.

"I was looking at your book. With the poems."

"That's OK. Did you like them?"

"They're different. He must have really liked his girlfriend."

I don't tell her that many of the sonnets were written for a man. Maybe in a few years.

"He was one of the greatest writers of all time. You'll read some of his plays and things. When you get in high school."

"Kayla?"

"What?"

"Did you get in trouble?"

"What do you mean?"

"At the beginning of practice. Your coach looked like he was mad at you."

"No, he wasn't mad. He was just explaining some things to me. Kind of grown up things. He can look pretty serious sometimes, though." I can't believe we're talking like this. What did this nice girl do with the evil Denise?

"Kayla? Will you show me how to wrestle?" Denise asks, a serious expression on her face.

"Really?"

"Yeah. It looks kinda fun. Is it?"

I think for a few seconds. "Yeah. It's pretty fun. But it's a lot of work, too. Hard work. OK, take your shoes off and come out here."

We walk onto the mat and I show her a couple of moves. A stand up, a switch and a takedown. All the guys have left, but I see Coach Pettus watching from the corner. He's smiling. I let Denise take me down and she helps me back up.

"OK, it's time to go. Your mom will have supper ready soon."

"Kayla? Do you think I could be a wrestler someday?"

I don't hesitate. "Sure you can. Any girl can do it. I'll teach you everything I know and…"

"You would?"

"Sure, why not?"

"Kayla?"

"What?"

"Thanks."

"For what?"

"Oh, nothing," she say. "Race you to the bikes!"

"OK, hang on a minute." I grab her arm and run by her. She squeals and catches up. I let her win the race.

We have a nice ride home. Talking. Almost like sisters.

CHAPTER TWENTY-SIX: OPHELIA'S LAMENT

I feel kind of sorry for the wrestlers who have to cut weight. Make that the guys who *choose* to cut weight. Coach says he would never force anybody to lose weight if they didn't want to. But we've only got fourteen on the team. That's a full team if everybody fits into a weight class. Coach P says that once you commit to a weight class, it's your job to make weight. You owe it to your teammates.

Wrestlers are really funny about weight. Before this year, I would never have asked anyone how much they weigh. But it's an everyday topic in the barn. Guys will ask, "How much are you over?" And everybody knows what it means. Nobody asks me that question. Not because I'm a girl, but because I've never been over my weight class. No matter what I eat, I always weigh around 104 or 105 pounds. My weight class is 106 now and it will go up to 108 in January. Something called a "weight allowance". Guess I'll need to eat a bunch over the holidays to fatten myself up. As grueling as practices are, I don't seem to have much fat. I'm as toned and strong as I've ever been in my life. It's a nice feeling.

But sitting at lunch with the guys, I feel a little weird eating in front of Bao and Calvin and Arthur. Sometimes they will eat just an apple. Maybe some yogurt or trail mix. Sometimes they don't eat lunch at all. Or drink anything. When they are getting desperate. I asked Bao once how he could stand sitting at the table watching everybody around him eat. He said that he got vicarious pleasure from seeing us eat whatever we want. A little bizarre, but OK.

Hollis asks me what I brought for lunch today. I actually forgot to pack a sandwich this morning. But as I'm riding through town, the woman from the furniture store stops me to talk for a minute. Found out her name is Mrs. Walker. She asks me what kind of furniture I like and what kinds of designs and patterns. Maybe she's taking a survey of what to stock in her store. But if so, why ask a kid? Just as I'm leaving, she pulls out a bag of bagels. I can tell they're the good kind. Like we'd get in Chicago. Not grocery store bought. She asks if I want one and then spreads it with maple walnut cream cheese. That's my lunch today. But when Hollis asks what I brought today, I tell him, my favorite, Pad Thai. He has no idea what Pad Thai is and Bao thinks that is hilarious. I explain that Thai food is my favorite, but that I'm actually eating a bagel. He nods his head as if I've just explained to him one of the great secrets of the universe. This table can be pretty weird at time. But it's our kind of weird. The good kind of weird.

After lunch, I've got English. Mr. C told us that we're going to start working with our partners today. Start writing our sonnets. Great. Forty-five minutes with just Madison and me. I'm tempted to ask if I can just bang my thumb with a hammer instead. But I don't think he'd go for it.

Mr. C splits up the groups and sends us out to various places to work. Sends Madison and me to the library and it is one deafeningly quiet walk down there. That's no hardship for me. At least she's not ripping on something about my appearance or whatever. When we get to the room and sit, Coach Pettus walks by. He sees me inside and signals for me to meet him in the hall. I tell Madison to just get started and walk out to meet him. He walks us around the corner.

"Just wanted to check if you're doing OK," he says.

"I'm fine. Why?"

"I was a little tough on you in practice the other day. About your decision to stay on. You've been kind of quiet since then."

"No, I'm OK. Sometimes I just think about things a lot and I was…"

"I know. You've had a lot going on. A lot to think about."

"Sometimes I think my brain is going to explode." I laugh.

"Well, don't stress too much about it. Just relax and have fun. With the sport and school and your life and everything. Being a kid should be fun."

"That's what my parents told me all the time. But they aren't…" I stop myself. Can't go there.

"Just remember. You've got people here now. People who care about you. People who are here to help you. You hear what I'm saying?"

I nod and look back toward the library

"OK, get back to class. See you after school."

"Bye," I say and round the corner. Back into the library. Madison sits near the back. She has her head on the desk in her arms. As I approach, I can hear her crying softly.

"What's wrong?" I ask.

"What do you care?"

"Well, if you're crying, you're gonna have a tough time writing a sonnet. What's going on?"

She pauses for a minute and looks at me through her tears. Her mascara has started to run and she looks vaguely like a female Alice Cooper.

"Nothing," she sobs. "I don't want to talk about it." She begins to cry in earnest. Again. "And I can't write a stupid sonnet. I have no idea what to write or how to write it. I hate this assignment."

"I can help you with the sonnet," I say. "But first, I want to ask you a question." I figure I can get this out of her when she's let her guard down. And no Raven around. "Why do you hate me so much?"

"Hate you? What are you talking about?"

"You've treated me like some kind of weirdo outsider ever since I started at this school. You know you have. So just tell me. Why do you hate me?"

"I don't hate you." She sniffs, but the thin line of snot finds its way out her left nostril anyway. "If anything, I'm jealous of you."

I snort. "What? Why on earth would you be jealous? Of me?"

"Are you really that clueless?"

I guess I am, because I have no idea what she's talking about. I ask again. "Why would you be jealous of me? My life hasn't been all fun and games the last few months."

Now it's Madison's turn to laugh. And it's not pretty. "Let me give you a couple of reasons why I might be jealous, if you really can't figure it out. You've been places. And you're going to go places. You're just taking a couple of years' pit stop in this crummy town."

"I still don't get it."

"You have no idea how good you've had it. You're from Chicago. You're smart. You're sophisticated. Yeah, don't smile. You're pretty sophisticated compared to the kids around here. You're gonna go to college. Probably get a scholarship. Move out of this town to someplace cool and you'll never look back. You'll forget about all of this." She waves her hand indicating the school and town. "In the blink of an eye."

"But you can get out of here too," I say. If you want to."

She laughs. It isn't a happy laugh.

"You have no idea. You really don't. See, this time in high school will be the best time in my life. In this place, for a couple of years, I'm the cool kid. Hanging with other cool kids. But college? Forget it. I'll be stuck in this…place for the rest of my life. Crappy job, no money, bunch of bratty kids, married to somebody like Donnie…ugh. I've seen it a million times."

"But you could change that. You could…"

"You don't realize how good you've had it." She sounds middle-aged already. "Compared to us.

Most of the kids here."

Suddenly I'm feeling a little sick. I can feel my face go red. But I'm gonna hang in here.

"OK. Fair enough. You answered my question. Thanks for being so honest. Now let's look at this sonnet stuff. It's really not that hard. First, what do you want to write about? Lots of sonnets are love-related. Do you want to write something about Donnie?"

"Oh God, no," Madison says.

"Trouble?"

"Yeah. And I don't want to talk about it."

"OK." Here goes nothing. "But if you ever do. Want to talk. I'll talk to you about it."

Madison looks at me. She's stunned. "You would? Huh."

I change the subject. "So you remember we've talked about iambic pentameter in class. You know, like ten syllables, stressed and unstressed? So, how about this for an opening line? 'My boyfriend Donnie can be such a jerk.'"

She laughs. "Did you just think that up?"

"Yep. I know you'll think this is weird. But when my Dad was in a Shakespeare play a couple of years ago, I went around talking in iambic pentameter for like two weeks straight. Drove my friends crazy."

She laughs again and says, "I can see why."

I can't believe I'm sitting here talking about my Dad and Shakespeare with Madison Bell. God, can things get any weirder around here?

"Now let's see if we can write the next couple of lines." I pull out a tissue and hand it to her. She wipes her eyes, then takes out her pen. To write. Thinks for a minute and counts with her fingers.

Sits up straight and says, "He treats me bad and my feelings are hurt."

"Nice job! See how easy it is?"

We work steadily until a kid from class summons us back. Madison's sonnet is finished and it's actually pretty good. And heartfelt, for sure. She wrote almost all of it herself. I'll write mine in my head when I ride to practice this afternoon. It's fun to think in sonnets. I remember Dad in his tights, and I smile.

CHAPTER TWENTY-SEVEN: CAMPING WITH LAURENCE

Christmas here in Felton was kind of a bittersweet time. My first without Mom and Dad. I cried, just a little, when I thought about them on Christmas morning. The day was pretty low key. I had told Arvin and June not to get me anything. I know how tight their money is. Whatever they've got should go to presents for the kids. They did buy me a couple of things. My own headgear (a cool, dark blue Cliff Keen brand) and a pair of fancy wrestling shoes. Asics brand, also blue. I told them that they shouldn't have gotten me anything. June told me privately that her friend Griff got the sports stuff wholesale. So I feel better about that.

I bought Denise a book at the school book fair. For Geneva, I got a little stuffed bunny. She said that her bunny was my Bun-Bun's baby. I gave Junior a sling shot. He loved it. But June warned that if she caught him shooting at any birds, animals or people she would paddle his behind. I'm sure she would make good on that promise.

We still had practice every day. A couple of the guys were gone. Off visiting family, I think. But most of us trudged through the snow every day to wrestle for a couple of hours. Arvin even came home from work one day to take me over to practice in his truck. So I wouldn't have to ride my bike.

The Christmas break was mostly that. Just a break. I stayed up late reading. Slept in. Didn't do any of the homework I hate. Like algebra.

But there was one day out of the two weeks that was pretty special. On that day, June and Arvin packed us all up to visit a friend of Arvin's a couple of counties over. Arvin and June sat in the front of the truck and the kids and I rode in the back. Bundled up with heavy blankets. Geneva sat on my lap the whole way. My job was to make sure that Junior and Denise didn't stand up. I know. No seat belts and dangerous and all. But it's just how people do things around here. We went way out in the country. To a gorgeous farm with a forest behind it. Rolling hills all covered with white. We hiked through the woods and saw eight or nine deer.

I tried to count, but they ran away too fast, their white tails bouncing through the bare trees. The kids and I sledded down hills, skated on a frozen pond, and drank hot chocolate out of an old fashioned thermos. I got into a crazy snowball war with Junior. Pegged him with a good one once and he did this dramatic ten-second fall into the snow. He can be pretty funny sometimes. It was like stuff people do in a Norman Rockwell painting. A year ago, I would never imagine myself saying this. But it was fun. Really, really fun.

When it got dark, we had supper (now they have me saying it) in the farmhouse of Arvin's friend. There was turkey and ham and mashed potatoes and homemade noodles and green beans and corn and biscuits and coconut cake for dessert. I might end up needing to cut weight after all. Luckily, no wrestling meets till school starts again.

After dinner, we all gathered around an old player piano. I had never seen one before. You feed this spool into some holes, start pushing these pedals and a song just plays. Like magic. We sang a bunch of them. They taught me *Back Home Again in Indiana*. A nice song. I liked it. Before we went home, we roasted marshmallows and made s'mores around a huge bonfire. Even in the back of the pickup, the kids and I slept the whole way home. It was one of those magical days that you remember for a long time. And it was a happy one. That's a nice change.

My first meet after break is at Green Ridge. It's Saturday, so June packs up Junior and Denise to see me wrestle for the first time. Hope I don't let them down. I've got a tall kid to wrestle. He's really skinny. First period, we circle each other for a long time. Nobody takes a shot. Finally, the ref stops the match and pulls us both together in the center of the mat. Talks to us privately. That's never happened to me before. The ref says, "C'mon guys. Help me out here. If I don't see some action soon, I'm gonna hit you both with a stalling penalty. I really don't want to do that." He looks at each of us separately and we both nod. Then blows the whistle and we start again. I fake high and then shoot a double. I'm in on both of his legs, but he sprawls hard. The pressure is too much and I feel my hands slipping.

Coach yells "Bail!" and I do. Back out from

under the guy, while holding one of his hands. Keep the hand on the ground so he can't grab me with it. Work my way back to standing and right away he shoots for my legs. So I've got to do the same thing he did earlier. Kick my legs out hard and crossface him. Pressure his cheek and nose with my arm. Technically, my radius bone. It hurts me, so I know it hurts him worse. He grunts under me and I see him grimace. So I know it's working. Gradually, I slip out of his grip. My feet are out of bounds, but he's still in. Coach is almost over my shoulder. "Hold him, right there," he orders, almost in my ear. I do and the buzzer sounds. First period over and I hear a smattering of cheers from the crowd. I make out Junior's voice.

Second period. The boy chooses down and I take my position. Look over at Coach and he tells me to switch to the other side. I do, but when the whistle blows I jump sides and it really throws the guy off. I break him down and put in an arm bar. Start to push him over and the ref warns, "Keep it legal." I push for about ten seconds and he's not budging. I need more pressure. So I push with both legs, taking a large step toward his head. Feel my arm slipping out of position. Higher. Onto his shoulder. The ref blows his whistle and grabs my arm, preventing me from pushing the boy's arm up any higher. Then puts his hand behind his head and says "Potentially dangerous." The ref stopped my hold before I could hurt the kid's shoulder. Coach always says a referee's main job is to keep the wrestlers from hurting each other. We start from the referee's position again. The boy is down on all fours and I'm on top and slightly behind him. One arm on his elbow and my other around his waist. On his naval. Whistle blows and I extend my the hand further around his waist. He's so skinny that I can reach halfway up his rib cage. Turn hard with my right arm and break down his elbow with my other arm. He goes down to the mat, but not over. Nowhere near his back. No points for me. We finish the second period the same way we started. The score is zero-zero.

"C'mon, Kayla, let's get out of there," Coach P encourages. He points down, and I assume the bottom position for the third period. It's easier to score from the bottom. The kid's got a good ride going. He does something we've worked on a little in practice. Throws one of his legs around one of mine and drapes himself over my back. The move is called "the legs" and it's pretty easy to see why. They hold you down with their legs. Nothing happens though. I can't get out, but he can't turn me over. We go out of bounds with 36 seconds to go.

"Kayla!" I look up to see Coach leaning over me. When the other kid walks back to the center, Coach shows me the fingers on one of his hands being pulled up by the fingers on his other hand. I nod and jog back to the center. We've been working on this technique really hard the past week. Coach wants it to be our go-to escape move. When the whistle blows, I put my head down on the mat. Immediately dig in the fingers of my right hand under his fingers around my waist. His fingers come out easily and I control his hand. Stand up fast with his hand away from my torso. Turn and face him. I'm out. The ref signals one point escape and the boy immediately shoots for a single leg takedown. He's got my leg. Twenty seconds to go.

Coach yells "Whizzer" and Calvin stands behind him yelling the same thing. I lace my right arm through his arm. The one holding my leg. Lean into him hard. Pressure down with my shoulder. Push his head down at the same time. Coach yells, "Hold it! Right there!"

My teammates count from the bench. "Four, three, two, one!" The buzzer sounds. I've won. 1-0. A lot of work for such a close win. I shake the boy's hand, the ref raises my hand and I turn to run to our bench. Coach points to the other team's bench and I turn. Run back across the mat and shake their coach's hand. He pats me on the back and says, "Nice job, young lady."

I say, "Thanks" and run back to our bench. High fives down the line. I wish I could say the rest of the meet went that well. But that would be lying. Stefano and Calvin got wins. But nobody else. The final score reads 51-12. Another opportunity lost. After we shake hands with their team, I look into the stands. June stands toe to toe with another woman. They are both clearly angry. I hear June shout: "Keep your cotton pickin' opinions to yourself! That's my girl out there." A man pulls the woman away from June. June never looks away from her as the woman is pulled back across the row of seats. Stares at her like a poisonous snake. Junior and Denise ignore the scuffle. Like they've seen it a million times before. I leave her to it and walk off with the team.

After the match, I shower and change in the Green Ridge girls locker room. Then Hollis drives me back to Felton. Kenna Faye has invited me to spend the night, so he drives me straight to her house. Well, not a house exactly. More like a trailer. What they call a double wide around here. Kenna Faye greets me at the door. I walk in and my nose is assaulted. "Sorry about the smell," Kenna Faye apologizes. "Gypsy had a litter a couple of weeks ago." We walk back to their kitchen and little things scurry everywhere. Too many to count. Puppies! Some yellow ones and some black ones. Gypsy lies on the floor panting. Looks like she's smiling. I'd be smiling too if I got all of those puppies out of me. Kenna Faye reaches down and picks up a yellow one. Hands it to me and the tiny thing snuggles against my cheek. Then licks my face. Over and over and over. Both of us erupt in laughter. We settle in on the kitchen floor and play with the pups for an hour.

CHAPTER TWENTY EIGHT: WHEN DOROTHY OPENS THE DOOR

I stay at Kenna Faye's house all day Sunday. It's kind of fun just hanging out with a girl for a while. I love my teammates. But they are boys. High school boys. Boys who think that gross jokes and burps and pushing each other down before practice is hilarious. Just like any other high school boys. When it comes time to get serious though, they are all business.

After a day of playing board games, looking at magazines, playing with the puppies and putting make-up on each other, Kenna Faye asks her Mom if I can stay for dinner.

"Sure, baby," her Mom says. "Just let me call over to June's to see if it's OK."

"We always do something funky for supper on Sunday," Kenna Faye explains. Her Mom comes back in and says it's OK if I stay.

"But they want you back home right after

supper," Mrs. Stephens says. Her voice is weak and she sounds tired. Like she's walked up Mt. Everest.

"Can we do tacos and popcorn and shakes for dinner, Mom?" Kenna Faye asks, obviously very excited by the prospect.

"No baby, we don't have the fixins for tacos. But we can do a grilled cheese instead. We got some Jiffy's and I can make you girls up chocolate shakes. That OK?"

Kenna Faye looks at me and we say "Sure" at the same time, then laugh hysterically. Her Mom stares at us dully.

So, we eat our sandwiches and popcorn while Mrs. Stephens sits on the back porch smoking. Out the smeared window, I watch her. She looks into the sky as a huge flock of sparrows flies overhead. A little late for migration. Black clouds roll overhead and the first couple of raindrops fall. She ignores the rain. Smoking away.

After we throw away our paper plates and clean up the kitchen, Kenna Faye fishes her Mom's keys out of her purse. Leans out the back door. "I'm gonna run Kayla home." Her Mom just waves her hand without looking back. Stares at the clouds as the rain gets stronger.

We pull up to my house and I start to get out. Kenna Faye touches my arm and says, "Hold on a sec." I close the door. Don't want to spend any more time in the rain than I have to. "I know your birthday is not until Tuesday, but I wanted to give you this." She hands me a bright yellow card. I open it and read. *To the first person in school who noticed that I exist. You've saved my life. In more ways than one. Love, KF.* Out of the greeting card, something plastic tumbles to the floor. I reach down and grab it. An I-Tunes gift card. For $25.

"Thank you so much, Kenna Faye," I say. "You didn't need to do this."

"I wanted to do this," she says, her face brightening. "You're my friend. My best friend. And thanks to you, I have other friends now."

"Yeah, we both do. And Kenna Faye?" Should I say it? "I don't mean to sound like I don't appreciate this. Because I really do. But I don't have an Apple. I don't have an Apple…anything."

She looks at me. A strange expression on her face. Like she's trying to decide something.

Finally says something after a long pause "Just take it. You never know."

I reach across the seat and give her a hug. She holds on for a few seconds, then lets me go. "You better get in. I was supposed to bring you straight home after supper. And I don't want to get on June's bad side."

"You and me both, sister." We both laugh. I hop out of the car with my card. Pull my jacket up to keep my head dry. Wave goodbye and walk up the front steps of the house. Cross the porch, open the front door and…something is going on. Something weird. Everyone is in the front room. June, Arvin and all the kids. Arvin wears his painting clothes. He looks like an artist's palette. The kids seem nervous. Super excited. And June has…is that a smile on her face? Like I said, definitely something weird going on.

Everyone stares as I walk in. Shaking some rain off my jacket. Should have done that on the porch. Arvin breaks the silence. "There you are, girl. Have fun over at your friend's?"

"Yeah, it was great." They're all just staring at me. Am I in trouble? I don't remember doing anything.

Junior squirms in his seat like he has to pee. He looks at June, then Arvin, then back at June. Finally he can't stand it any longer. Says in a loud whisper, "When are we gonna..." His voice gets just a hair quieter. "...tell her?" June shushes him and Arvin stands. What the hell is going on here?

"Boy, leave Kayla be. She probably wants to get up to her room and do homework." OK, that's a little strange. They never have to remind me to do my homework. But I do have homework to do. Since I'm dismissed, I walk out of the room. Around the corner to the stairs and climb. When I reach the landing at the top, I hear footsteps behind me. Junior and Denise have followed me up the stairs. Are they getting ready to prank me again? Junior ever so slightly points to the right and Denise jabs him in the ribs.

My gaze follows the direction of his finger. Look to my end of the hall and something is not right. What is that? A spiral staircase? Leading up to my room in the attic. "What's going on?"

Junior laughs and then Denise joins in. Junior prods. "Go up and look."

I walk to the staircase and examine it. Really pretty. I've always thought spiral staircases were cool, but how did this get here? When? The frame of the staircase is a gleaming black metal. Shiny and smells like fresh paint. The stairs are blue and white, alternating colors with each step. I get it. Felton High School colors. I turn to the kids. "Where did this come from?"

"Daddy and them…" Junior starts, but this time it's Denise's turn to shush him. "Go on up and look," he blurts. As excited as I've ever seen him. I take the steps slowly. Like Dorothy taking her first few on the Yellow Brick Road. Run my hand over the railing as I walk up. While it's shiny and bright, it's not slick. Wonder how they did that?

At the top of the staircase, there is a small landing and a door. That door wasn't here yesterday morning when I left. I open the door and walk in. The Dorothy analogy still works, because I feel like I'm looking into Oz. It's…it's magical. My room has been transformed. The drab and functional place I lived in before is gone. In its place is like something out of *1001 Nights*. Like a Bedouin tent. It's hard to take it all in. First, my bed. It's been moved in front of the window and ...wait that's not my bed. In place of my steel-framed hospital-type bed is one built up on a platform. No frame or box spring. The platform is trimmed in lush orange fabric wrapped around the length of the platform and extending onto the headboard. Above the headboard is a sleek movable reading light. Like something from Ikea. The bedding is done in a wild combination of patterns—purples and yellows and whites and more orange. Sprinkled here and there with multicolored daisies. At the head of the bed is an assortment of pillows. Two match the comforter and two are in a complementary orange. Two more big pillows sit on the floor. This is wild.

Draped around the headboard and extending up and out to the curved ceiling is a tent-like canopy. Solid orange on the outside, splashed with patterns of purples, yellows and deep reds. At the top of the canopy hangs a multi-pointed, three dimensional silver star. A night light of sorts. Junior turns off the overhead light and the star throws wild, undulating fingers of light across the ceiling. He flips the light back on and I notice the ceiling for the first time. Every inch of the slanted attic rook is covered with billowy multi-hued fabrics. Some hug the ceiling tight, while others drape down at a variety of levels. Very artistic. Over the window, they've put in a Roman shade. Done in patterns that match the canopy.

I follow the slanted walls down to the floor. It's been lacquered in luscious colors, a deep red hue which appears purple when you look at it another way. I'm reminded of a cool dress my Mom used to wear. She called it *couleur changee.* I follow the floor to the place where my bed used to be and gasp. On the far end of the wall is a miniature roll top desk, refinished in a light oak stain. Like the color of toffee candy. All of my books are stacked neatly at the top of the desk, sitting between light oak bookends that match the desk. I squeal when I look at the center of the desk. Yes, literally squeal. And I'm not the squealing type. In the center of the desk sits a laptop. The top of the laptop is decorated with patterns that match the bedding. Oh. My. God. So that's what the I-Tunes card is for. How did she…?

I look back to the door and Junior and

Denise have disappeared. A knock at the door and it's Arvin. "Can we come into your...how do you say it June? 'Bud' something?"

"Boudoir," June corrects.

"Please do," I say. "Come into my boudoir."

"Well, girl, what do you think?"

"It's... it's just..." I can't finish because I'm crying. Run to Arvin and give him a big hug. He seems tentative, so I back off. "You guys. I love it. With a capital 'L.' This is so cool, but how did you...why? Oh crap, this is way too expensive. When did you do this?"

Arvin looks around and smiles. "Yesterday and today. Had a few guys helping me out. I help them sometimes and they help me. We salvaged a few things. Staircase from a house they were tearing down in town. Ms. Walker from the furniture store gave us a few things. She had that old roll top in her attic. Just gathering dust up there. So she cleaned it up some. Did all these drapes and what not too. She used to be an artist."

I thought this had an artist's touch.

"And what about the laptop? That is just too much. Too expensive and..."

June stops me. "That was from Griff. Said a girl smart as you needs a computer these days. Got that one from some place that fixes them up. Says it's a good one though. He knows that kind of stuff. He covered all the other costs too."

"But we don't have cable or anything here. How can I…" Damn, I'm getting greedy. Stop it.

"Well that's a good question," Arvin says. "The Millers next door saw us carryin' all this stuff in. Told 'em what we were doin' and they had an idea. They got one of them hi fi things…"

"Wi-fi," Junes corrects.

"Yeah, one of them. They got a pretty good signal, so they said you can just piggy back off of theirs. Tested it out and danged if it didn't work. They wrote their secret code down on a paper. It's under your computer. So, happy birthday, gal. Couple days early."

"This is the best birthday present ever. Thanks, you guys. And I want to write down the names of everybody that helped. I can babysit or whatever they want to pay them back. After the season's over."

"Don't worry about that." He yawns and

stretches. "I got to get to bed. We worked till about 4 a.m. this morning. I ain't been up that late since…"

"Arvin Spurling, you ain't never been up that late," quips June.

He laughs. Says "goodnight" and walks out the door. June starts after him and I call her. "June, can I ask you something?"

"What's that, girl."

"Who is this Griff guy? Why would he do all this for me? When he doesn't even know me."

"Griff knows me."

"But who is he? What is he to …" I think the word 'you', but don't go there. Maybe something I don't want to know.

"I know what you're askin'. I was raised foster. Just like poor Mr. Richmond's kids and quite a few other kids here in town. My Mama died when I was about Denise's age. Daddy took to drinkin'. Drinkin' heavy. Wasn't no way he could take care of a little girl. So Griff and his wife took me in and raised me. She died a ways back and he's all alone now."

"But why is helping me out? He doesn't

even know me."

"Griff has helped Arvin and me out whenever things got tight over the years. He sort of adopted all of us. He feels like…if you're part of our family, then he wants to help you too."

"That's really nice."

"Yeah, he is a good sort. Griff told me the other day that you remind him of me when I was a teenager. Kind of scrappy and not afraid to mix it up with the boys." She looks away and laughs to herself. "I'm goin' to bed too. And you done OK in that fight on Saturday."

I don't correct her. "What was Emerson yellin' at you? Was he calling you a 'wizard'?"

My turn to laugh. "No. He was telling me to use a 'whizzer'. It's a wrestling move."

"Huh," she says and grabs the door handle. "Night, girl."

"Good night. And thanks again. For all of this." She closes the door behind her and her shoes clack down the staircase. My staircase.

I walk to the bed and see that my bunny is tucked in between two of the pillows.

"Hi Bun-Bun. What do think of all this?" I

hold him up and let him look around the room. He approves.

"What's that Bun?" I move him next to my ear.

"I agree. Life is full of surprises. And not all of them are bad."

CHAPTER TWENTY-NINE: THE PICKWICK CLUB

As a team, we've been talking about the upcoming meets. At the end of practice. Just us wrestlers. We had meets against Morrisville, Rushton, and Bartsville. We knew none of them would be easy. And now they are behind us. Three more lost opportunities to win one. For Coach. For the team. For the school. For our pride. But mostly for Coach. Win a meet and we become a school team. Become a school team and he gets a job as a teacher and coach. His family can afford to join him here. Be together again. There's so much riding on us. It scares me.

Now, it's down to our meet with Sheffield. I've heard so much about how good Sheffield is. I'm sick of hearing about them. They all say we don't have a chance against them. And Calvin told me the other day that their 106 pound guy is their best wrestler. When I heard the name, I couldn't believe it. Rick Gray. The boy who was scraping the floor at the bakery the night June and I went in. The one who wouldn't even look at me, much less talk to me. He must have known who I am. But why would he care about me? I'm no threat to a guy like him. At least that's what I'm picking up from the guys.

The *big day* approaches. That's right. Just three days till the Sheffield meet. Can't wait until it's over. I just want the pressure off.

We're working on writing in different genres in English class. Last week, it was description. I wrote a short paper describing everything I could see, hear, taste and smell in a clear glass of pop. I know technically, it was a brand of pop, but old habits die hard. This week we're moving on to journalism reporting. Since you should write what you know, I decided to write about the last two weeks of my life. So here's goes:

Members of Felton Wrestling Club Travel to Sheffield

Four members of the Felton High school wrestling club traveled to nearby Sheffield January

11 for a day of entertainment. Organizing the trip were sophomore student Hollis Fleming and junior Arthur Boxell. Accompanying the organizers were freshmen Kayla Burbadge and senior captain of the club Calvin Sweet. After preliminary stops for brownies and donuts at Gray's Bakery, the club members traveled to The Root Beer Spot, a dining establishment informally known as "The Stand". Ms. Burbadge pronounced the event a "rockin' good time" and announced that the "Hurry-up Burgers at the The Stand were pretty much the bomb." According to Fleming, "We have a pretty good time like this just about every Saturday." No report if a return visit is planned.

Student Loses One Home; Finds Another

Felton high school senior James "Jimmy" Dole (19) was saddened last month by the untimely death of his foster mother, Pauline Richmond (age 53). But further tragedy befell Dole as his foster father Ralph Richmond (54) announced that he was no longer able to continue housing Dole and two other foster children, Donald Allen (13) and Trevor Johns (12). "I just don't have the time and money *to keep up all them kids. What with Pauline gone," announced a heartbroken Mr. Richmond. But Dole's tragedy was lessened this week when it was announced that Felton High School janitor and wrestling club coach Emerson Pettus offered to assume the responsibility of caring for Dole through the remainder of his senior year. "I don't need anybody to take care of me. I'm not some kid," reported a relieved Dole. "Just a bed and roof is all." Reports indicate that Mr. Dole plans to enlist in the United States Marine Corps after receiving his high school diploma from Felton Senior. "I'm not having that boy drop out," announced a stern- faced Pettus. "Getting that diploma is a condition of his staying with me." Pettus reported further that the diploma requirement is "non-negotiable".*

Debutante Hosts Exotic Slumber Party

Miss Kayla Burbadge, age 15 and a freshman at Felton High School, had a problem. A gorgeous new room and nobody to share it with. "I absolutely adore what they've done with the place. I mean my place," said Burbadge, beaming at her newly redecorated attic bedroom. The lovely space, designed in an exotic Moroccan theme, was just too much fun to keep to herself. But the inventive young Burbadge had a plan. With the help of the younger members of her household, Burbadge arranged the Spurling home's first-ever slumber party. Joining Miss Burbadge for the festivities were 11-year-old Denise Spurling, 9-year-old Arvin Spurling Junior and 4-year-old Geneva Spurling. According to the youngest Spurling child, the event was "So...much...fun!" While Arvin Junior asked that the family's pet blue tic hound dogs, Tige and Prince, be included in the festivities, family matriarch June Spurling vetoed that notion. "Ain't no way I'm havin' them dogs runnin' wild all over this place. When they do their business on the floor, you can guess who'll be cleaning it up!" Dogs or no dogs, the soiree was judged by the party-goers to be an unqualified success. Guests were served a smorgasbord of hot dogs, chips, orange Fanta and leftover birthday cake. After a rousing game of Candyland, won by Arvin Junior, the attendees retired to Miss Burbadge's lovely, tent-style bed for a reading hour. "'Little Women' was boring," reported Arvin Junior. "Except for that part where the girl almost drowned. That was cool." The older Spurling girl disagreed. "I like the Jo girl. She just does what she wants and doesn't care what other people think about her." After the reading hour, Arvin Junior and Denise retired to sleeping bags on the floor, while Geneva joined Miss Burbadge for a snuggle in the bed, followed by lights out at 10:30. "It was really fun," Miss Burbadge quipped, on reflection. "Maybe we'll do it again this summer. In a tent in the back yard." All participants concurred: a good time was had by all.

Poll Results Mixed on Felton High Lunch Quality

According to a recent, non-scientific poll conducted in the Felton High School Cafetorium, students reported mixed feelings regarding the quality of the food served at the school. According to the poll, one student found the food "Pretty awful, but what do you expect?" Sophomore James Rockman stated that he had low expectations for the food, so did not consider the quality issue to be significant. Rockman added, "Good job this year

Kayla. Hope you guys kick Sheffield's ass."

A second student, junior Penny Tripp, had no opinion. "I bring my lunch every day. So I don't know. Hey, aren't you that girl wrestler?" Finally, senior football player Richard Shell had this to say, "I had the breaded tenderloin and it was pretty good. You know, my little sister thinks it's cool that you wrestle. She's telling my parents that she wants to wrestle in high school. It freaked them out. So…awesome!" Final poll results show one favorable opinion, one unfavorable and one no opinion. In the estimation of this researcher, more study is required in this important aspect of student nutritional well-being.

Felton Wrestling Club Stumbles Toward End of Season

Entering the current season, the Felton High School Wrestling Club had a single team goal. One win. While most teams would consider this a modest accomplishment, the Felton Club has more at stake. According to team co-captain Stefano Mendez, "We need this win. For Coach and his family. We're going to get them all together in

Felton. Finally." Unfortunately, the single win required to establish a permanent wrestling team, with Emerson Pettus installed as Coach and physical education teacher at the school, has been elusive. Entering the final stretch of the season, their opponents have dominated the determined wrestling club. In recent dual meets, Felton has fallen 42-24 to rival Rushton, with Morrisville defeating the club 62-16. The club lost a heartbreaker on the road to Bartsville 36-32. According to newcomer Kayla Burbadge, the team's lone female competitor and one of the few girl wrestlers in Indiana, "We're just sick about this. We've got to get Coach his win. But time is running out." Burbadge reported that her own winning record of seven wins versus five losses is little solace. "I don't care about that," she responded firmly. "We've got to win one as a team. It's all that matters." When asked to comment on the team's chances against state powerhouse Sheffield, Burbadge bristled, "I'm tired of hearing about how good they (Sheffield) are. I'm just ready to go out and beat them."*

Sheffield is 18-2 on the season, led by state-

ranked junior 106 pound team captain, Rick Gray, who sports a record of 19-1. The dual meet between the teams is scheduled for 6:00 p.m. on Thursday, January 24, at the William Garrett gymnasium in Sheffield.

Breaking News:

Sheffield Cancels Final Meet;

Facility Conflict Spells End of Felton Wrestling Season

Oh…my…God.   It's   all   over.

CHAPTER THIRTY: MAKING PEACE

My Dad used to play this dumb game with me. He'd ask if I wanted the good news or bad news first. I always chose bad news first and he knew that. So he had this whole corny spiel made up. Usually, there was no bad news. At least not really bad. So when Coach calls us together in the barn after school and says, "There's good news and bad news," I am ready.

"Bad news first, Coach," I chime in, and all the guys turn to stare at me.

"OK, Kayla." He smiles quickly, then gets serious. "Well, I'm sure most of you have already heard the bad news. Sheffield cancelled on us. They needed to make up a gymnastics meet. One that was postponed for weather. So they're using the gym for that. And their mats. Our meet's just exhibition, so we got pushed out."

"So, what's the good news, Coach?" Calvin asks, quietly, from the middle of our group.

"Well, I spent a lot of time on the phone last night. The bottom line is this. We're wrestling them. Tomorrow night. Here."

Lots of guys speak at once.

"Quiet down, everybody. So, here's what happened. Got a building inspector from the county to come in here yesterday. She checked out the barn and said we're good to go. Kind of rushed it through with the commissioners. We can only let 150 people in here, but that shouldn't be a problem. We'll get a couple of small bleachers for down here and maybe forty or fifty people can stand up above. Talked to the Sheffield Athletic Director too. They can do it, but they have to move it up a day. So…it's happening tomorrow. Six o'clock. They'll weigh in before coming and we'll do it over at school. We agreed to a morning weigh in." Cheers from around the room.

"That's right, Bao, you can eat lunch tomorrow. But guys, don't stuff yourselves. If any of you puke on my mat, you're cleaning it up yourself." Laughs all around. "So we'll do a light workout tonight. Talk about what I know Sheffield will do. Get a good night's sleep and come in here tomorrow ready to wrestle. OK?" Everybody agrees. "Kayla, can you wait outside for a minute. Some of the guys need to change." I nod and stand up. "You can wait in my truck. Stay out of the cold."

I step outside and the wind whips me against the barn. Damn it's cold. Nasty looking black clouds roll across the horizon. The lingering shafts of sunlight make the cornfield of the farm next door look like an old Dutch painting. It's beautiful and kind of ominous at the same time.

After practice, I accept a lift home with Hollis. It's too cold to ride my bike. Walk in the front door and everybody's gathered in the kitchen. Waiting for me. June speaks first, "Well they're all buzzing about it over at the bakery. Movin' that meet down here to the barn. Rick and some of the Sheffield boys aren't too happy about it." Poor Rick. We sure don't want him to be unhappy. June continues, "Do you want us to come over tomorrow? All of us?"

"Sure. But I don't know. He's supposed to be really good and …"

"Yeah, he is good," June offers. "But so

what? You just go out there and do your best. Whatever happens, happens."

"Yeah," says Junior. "Go out there and beat him up."

"I'm not beating anybody up. It's a wrestling match." Junior giggles and Denise joins in. Pretty soon, we're all laughing. Not sure what we're laughing about.

"If you guys want to go, you should get there early," I warn. "They're only letting 150 people in. But I don't know if anybody will come to see us."

June says, "Oh, you may be surprised."

Wouldn't be the first time. A quick dinner, then I head upstairs. After two weeks, I'm still surprised every time I see that spiral staircase. Can't believe I have such a cool room. My old friends from Chicago would just die. My old friends.

Climb under my comforter and snuggle up with Bun-Bun. "Tomorrow night, my furry friend. The big show. All the marbles. The whole enchilada." Bun-Bun looks at me and smiles. But then, he's always smiling. Lucky guy. Pick up

Little Women and read from where I left off with the kids. Continue on through Chapter 39 and stop. Next chapter is about what happens to little Beth, and that's just too depressing before bed. Reach up and click off my reading light. My star nightlight comes on overhead. Lights up in the dark, unless I pull the plug. Throws beams in every direction around my room. Like Pollyanna's prisms. I begin to drift.

Wake and check my clock. 6:45. Is it morning? I dream almost every night, but last night, nothing. Just sleep—almost 11 hours of the stuff. I feel different. Calm. Peaceful. But kind of excited. Not sure why. It's gonna be a bloodbath tonight. Metaphorically, of course.

All day at school, kids I pass in the hall say stuff about the match. Encouraging stuff. They announced it first period. Made a big deal out of it. Urged all the students to show up at the barn tonight. Support us. And now the whole place is buzzing. About us. It's a weird feeling. But I kinda like it. After third period, I look up to see Madison and Donnie walking. Right toward me. Just before they pass me, I see Madison pull Donnie's arm and they stop. Right in front of me. Madison says, "Hi Kayla." It's the first time she's ever said hi to me. What's going on now? "I just wanted to say good luck tonight. Everybody is talking about you guys. You're like, famous."

"Thanks," I say and start for class.

I get about five feet past them and hear "Kayla." It's Donnie. I turn and face him. What now? "Kayla, I wanted to… I thought. Oh nothing." I turn away and he continues. "Kayla, I just…" He looks down, then back up. Directly in my eyes. "Kick that Gray kid's ass. For all of us."

"I'll do my best." I say. He takes a step toward me and raises his hand. Wants a high five. I consider for a second and take one step toward him. Slap his hand, then turn and walk to class. Baby steps.   OK   for   now.

CHAPTER THIRTY-ONE: INTO THE GULLEY

Seems strange riding on a school bus with all the guys. It's like we're a real team. Coach arranged for the bus. And he's driving. So we'd all be together. Sheffield is warming up first—right now. It's snowing like crazy, but we know they made it here. Coach talks by cell with Principal Drake, who is in the barn. He's calling Coach back when they are done with warmups. Then we'll make our grand entrance. For our first home meet. There are definitely people here. In fact, a ton of them, judging from all the cars. The small parking lot is full and cars line the entrance drive and the county road leading up to it back for a quarter mile A few people see us drive in and they bang on the side of the bus. A few friendly waves, thumbs-ups and whistles. We pull up to a spot reserved for us and park. The motor idles and we wait in the bus. Where it's warm. It is frigid outside. I'm surprised to see it snowing so hard with the temperature in the single digits.

Coach P stands and faces us. "OK guys. In a couple minutes we're gonna go in. I'm not a big one for pep talks. But I want to ask just one thing. Do your best. Work hard for six minutes. Leave it all on the mat. And whatever happens, happens." Where have I heard that before? "Don't be psyched out by these guys. They're just high school boys. Like you guys." He looks at me and smiles. "Sorry, Kayla."

"No problem, Coach."

"So when we go in there, it's gonna be loud. Drake says the place is packed to the rafters. Yes, literally to the rafters." We all laugh. "But this is your house and..." His cell rings. He looks at the number and answers. "Right, OK, we're coming in. Thanks." Back to us. "This is your house. Our house. Go in there and own it." He steps to the front and pushes open the bus door.

Calvin and Stefano get up first, walk to the front and turn. Calvin says, "Ready guys?" and we all agree. Start down the steps and into the snow. There are twelve or fifteen people standing outside the barn door peering in. Must be over capacity. Oh crap. We jog toward the crowd. They see us and a cheer goes up. Spreads to the people inside the door and ripples through the stands. Calvin stops just outside the door and turns to us. "Wipe your shoes off on these towels before we go in." We all take turns. I feel several hands pat my back as I make my way forward. When all of our shoes are clean, Calvin nods at Stefano, who nods back. "Let's do this thing," he says seriously. We enter the barn running and a roar goes up. And they are cheering for *us*. I feel like I might lift off and fly to the ceiling.

We hit the mat and begin our jog. On the second lap around I sneak a glance at the Sheffield team. Know I'm not supposed to, but…and see him. Gray is laughing. Pointing at me and joking around with some teammate. I look away and continue jogging. Ignore the jerk, I tell myself, but it's hard to do. We jog, warm up and start drilling. The usual stuff. But I feel different. It's warm in here. The new heaters are really working. And all of these people. Warmer than normal. I feel…sick. Oh God. "Arthur, I've got to…" But I don't finish.

Run for the back door and throw it open. Sprint to the Portajohn and just make it in time. To throw up right behind it. Footsteps come up behind me. Fast. "Kayla." It's Jimmy Dole. He finds me behind the john. Helps me off my knees and brushes the snow off of them. "Are you OK?" Jimmy asks.

I stop and look up at him. Think of that line from *Pulp Fiction*. When Ving Rhames' character says: "I'm pretty damn far from OK." Only he used another adjective.

"I'll be alright." I do feel better now. Just a little something I had to get off my chest. Or out of my stomach. Jimmy hands me a water bottle and I take a pull. Swish it around in my mouth and spit it out. Then take a long drink. Offer him the bottle back and he pushes it away, laughing.

Jimmy says, "No thanks. You better keep it."

"You don't happen to have a breath mint, do you?"

He fake-pats his singlet and says, "Not on me. Besides, your breath is just about right now for that Gray guy. Wish he was in my weight class."

"I wish so too, Jimmy."

"Ready to go back?"

"Yep. What's that thing they say? In pro wrestling? Let's get ready to rumble?"

"Something like that." He leads the way to the back door. We both stamp our shoes and walk in. The temperature in the barn is about 60 degrees warmer than outside. Our warmups are finished. The two coaches talk on the side of the mat. I find my headgear and get loose. Fast. Behind our bench. As out of sight as I can be. Coach Pettus walks back to our bench and I start forward. Ready to rock and roll. Slap my legs, my arms and my headgear. My new little routine. Coach meets me before I reach the mat and takes my arm.

"We drew a weight out of a hat. We're starting at 113. Arthur, you're up." Arthur grabs his headgear and runs to the mat. I take his seat on the bench, next to Stefano. Turn to him and ask, "What just happened?"

"Oh that," he says, nonchalantly. I've never seen the guy get excited or worried about anything. I need some of that calm. "Coaches can just pick a weight and start anywhere. Mixes things up some."

"But what about my match?"

"You'll go last. After Hollis." I'm too stunned to think, let alone talk. I have to be the last one on the mat. Wait all that time. I look down to Hollis and he waves. I guess he does that every match. The waiting thing. I'm being a selfish baby. Not like my match will matter anyway. We'll be so far behind by then. The ref blows his whistle and Arthur's match begins. Look up. This is so surreal. Tons of people cheering from the balcony sections. Running along the top of the gym on three sides. It's wall to wall screaming and cheering in here. Not like some half empty high school gym.

Arthur's guy is pretty good. He loses 13-4. They get an extra point for that and we're down 4-0. Stefano's guy is even better. For the first time all season, he gets pinned. And in the first period. We're down 10-0. This is going about like everyone expected. Bao wrestles his best match of the season. He's ahead 16-1 in the second period and the ref stops the match. I look to Calvin and he anticipates my question. "Tech fall. Get up by 15 points and they stop the match." I learn something new every day. Emmy draws one of their top wrestlers. A state finalist last season. It's over in 23 seconds and we're down 16-5.

Then a weird thing happens. Mike Kotlowitz takes the mat. I can hear Sarah screaming like crazy behind me, but I don't look. He stands out there alone for a second and the ref looks to the Sheffield Coach. He signals forfeit and the ref raises Mike's hand. Calvin is next and the same thing happens. He trots back to the bench and sits next to me. "Why are they forfeiting?" I ask.

"Coach said flu's been going around their team," says Calvin. "He didn't want to tell everybody. In case they brought up some JV guys. Guess they think they can beat us without those matches." Going into Don's match at 152, we're leading 17-16. I can't believe it. We're actually beating Sheffield. Don wrestles well, but loses 5-4. Jaco May runs out at 160 and again, the ref raises our guy's hand. Forfeit number three. We're up again in team score 23-19. Then things get rough. Real rough. Ray gets pinned with a cradle move in 41 seconds. Dave Sperry's opponent puts him on his back with the same move. The ref slaps the mat and Sperry stomps off. Throws his headgear toward the back wall. The ref sees it and shouts: "That's one team point deduction from Felton." Coach glares at Dave, but stays with the team. We need his coaching. Jimmy's up next, with Sheffield leading 32-22. Three matches to go before mine. He walks off the mat smiling. That's been pretty rare this year. Jimmy smiling, that is. We cut their lead to 32-25. I do some math in my head. Nothing adds up.

If I'm being completely honest, Ernesto and Hollis are not our best wrestlers. Of course, I would never say that out loud. To anyone. But it's a fact. Bless their hearts. They try hard. Every day in practice. And they are nice kids. But they've got three wins between them all season. Two for Hollis and one for Ernesto. Ernesto wrestles his guy close for two periods. Very conservative. Nothing flashy. Thirty-one seconds to go in the match. Both wrestlers on their feet. Neutral position. The ref sees blood on the other guy's cheek and calls a timeout. To find and stop the bleeding.

"Ernesto, come here." Coach motions him over our sideline. Coach P whispers in his ear and demonstrates a hold on Jimmy Dole. Ernesto nods his head and Coach slaps him on the back. "Do it now," he says. "Don't wait." The ref calls them to the center. Checks the guy's face for blood and finds it satisfactory. Steps back and blows his whistle. Ernesto charges forward. He's about four inches taller than his opponent. Reaches over and tugs down on his head. The kid snaps his head back and stands straight up, leaving his legs undefended. Ernesto shoots for both of his legs and the kid goes down hard. The ref signals a 2 point takedown. Ernesto holds on the final eight seconds for the win. We're down 32-28. Hollis ambles out to the mat with Coach shouting at his back. "Go get him, big guy."

I can't watch this. Need some more air. Out the back door again and lean against the barn. Strangely, I can't seem to feel the cold. The back door opens and Arthur appears. He's smiling and jumping up and down. To stay warm. Walks up to me and assumes a wrestling stance. I laugh. "How you doin' Kayla?"

"On a scale of 1 to 10?" I ask. "I'd say a 3. Maybe 3.5."

"That's not bad. I thought you'd come up

with a negative number."

"Nah. I'm OK. But…do you have any advice?"

"You mean like sage Indian wisdom?"

"I'll take anything you got."

He thinks for a minute. "Here's my advice. Couple of things. Spend a little time and get really relaxed. In your head. Calm. Lose the stress. This is just a wrestling match. We're not solving world hunger in there. It's not life or death."

"But there's a lot…"

He cuts me short. "No buts. Just go out there and have fun. Second thing. Trust the wrestling that Coach has taught us. It's nothing fancy. But you know it. We've drilled it over and over and over. You have muscle memory now."

"Yeah, I seem to remember some of that drilling." We both laugh. The barn door pops open and Calvin peeks out. Stays off the snow, but peers around the door till he spots us.

"Kayla, the ref is calling 106."

CHAPTER THIRTY-TWO: BEAR ON FIRE

I open the barn door to the din. It's deafening. And I hear something really scary. But thrilling too. It's the crowd. They are chanting. Really loud and in unison: "Kayla!…Kayla!…Kayla!" When they spot me putting on my head gear and peeling off my warm-up, a huge cheer goes up. I've never been cheered for by a crowd. For anything. In my entire life. I try to put them out of my mind. Put everything out, except my wrestling moves. Like Arthur told me. I don't look at the bench. Or Hollis. Or Coach. Or the scoreboard. None of that is going to help me now. I'm on my own, for the next six minutes. I feel ready for that.

Gray stands on his line, waiting. Doesn't look in my direction. He seems bored. Run to the mat and my hand is out. "Good luck," I say.

He chuckles and whispers, "Right."

The ref steps back and blows the whistle.

We're on. I circle once and shoot for both legs. I'm in deep, with a good grip. But he sprawls hard. The laces of his wrestling shoes are all way down on the mat. He slides backward. Cross faces me. Hard. Damn, that hurts. Don't care though. Try to get in close on his legs, but he keeps sliding back. Back further. Then the ref blows his whistle.

"Out of bounds," he says.

"That's the way to work, Kayla! Stay on the offensive," Coach shouts from the sideline.

Gray grabs my head and arm and tries a throw. Trying to get this over with fast. Coach has drilled our defense for this. "What do you do when somebody tries to throw you?" he's asked. Seems like a million times. Then he shrugs. That's the joke. Shrug it off. I position my body on the opposite side of his throw and I shrug. My head is slipping out and quickly, I'm free. Gray turns quickly and I circle out—back to the center of the mat. I'm not letting him use the out-of-bounds line to his advantage.

Gray strikes again. Goes for his own double leg takedown and I defend it the same way he did. Sprawl as hard as I can. Shoe laces down and slide.

And I cross face him as hard as I can. My radius bone grinding into his cheek and nose. I keep the cross face working into the side of his face. Pushing harder with every second. If you're on the receiving end of a cross face, it feels a little like a slow, continuous punch to the face. Right now, I'm on the giving end. And I'm giving it all I've got. Since we started in the center, we eat a lot of the clock working to the sideline. I see my feet slide over the line, but we're still in bounds. We're nearly flat with me on top of him. I try to scoot behind him and he blocks with his left arm. Try the other side and he blocks with his right. Ref blows the whistle and we're out of bounds.

Eighteen seconds left in the first period. I look to the sideline and Coach taps his prosthetic leg. That's his signal to shoot a single leg takedown. When we start again I quickly tie up his head and work left, left, then left again. He takes the bait and moves against my pressure. Sweep down the other side and pull up his left leg. One of the keys to the move is get your opponent's leg up high. Leg higher, less balance. I'm a couple inches taller than Gray, so I'm going as high as I can. Feel him lose balance as he tries to back away from my grip. When I can't go any higher with his leg, I sweep his other leg out with mine. Land on top. He is completely out of bounds, but my toes are in bounds. Ref shouts, "Two, takedown." Hold right there for three seconds and the buzzer sounds. First period over. I'm up 2-0.

Second period and Gray says nothing when the ref asks position. Doesn't look at his coach. Just points down. He assumes the bottom position. I start on top. On his left side. At the whistle, pop my knee down on his ankle. I hear him suck in his breath. I just hold it there for a second. Then reach down with my right hand and grab his right ankle. Pull it up, while pushing down on his left arm at the elbow. The break down works and I hold him there for a second. But he's back to his base quickly. He hits a switch and I try to follow. Try again, but he has my arm and shoulder pinned down. It hurts. I go down to the mat and he pulls himself on top of me. Ref signals two points for a reversal. We're tied. Little more than a minute to go in the period.

Gray throws in the legs. Threads his right leg around my right leg and drapes himself over my back. The legs can be a very effective series of moves if used correctly. But dangerous if used incorrectly. Coach says that most of us are not ready to use them as an offensive weapon. So he teaches the defensive strategy against the hold. And we just went over it yesterday in practice. Before Gray can work any of his magic, I sit out hard. Put him on his side, with his leg still draped around mine. Dig my finger under his wrestling shoe and pull it out. We're in a weird position. No way I'm letting go of his shoe. And I keep scooting away from him and he keeps pulling me back in. Constant motion, so we're not in a stalemate position. With ten seconds left, he abandons the legs and goes for a traditional breakdown. Forces me down on the mat, but no pinning combination. The buzzer sounds again and we're on to the third and final period. Tied at 2-2.

I look over to Coach and he says, "What do you want to do?" He's never let me make my own position choice before. I kind of like that. I nod and walk back to the center. The ref looks me over and I point down.

Assume my bottom position. Ref asks,

"Bottom man ready? OK, hold that. Top man on." The second Gray assumes his position, the whistle blows. I hear Gray's knee hit the mat just like mine did in the last period. But I've already cleared my feet. Looking for a sit out and turn in move. But he follows and tight waists me hard. Looking for a tilt. I counter with pressure to the other side. I feel Gray reach under my neck and try to go over my head. Going for a ¾ nelson. Kind of a power move to cause the bottom guy's head to go down and force the shoulders to the mat. But I defend by arching my back and neck. Hard. I push back into him. Get my feet underneath me and push up. My shoulder against his upper body and my hips away. But he pulls me in and lifts me up off the mat. In one fast, hard motion I hit the mat. Hard. I hear myself say "ooof" and then feel it. I can't breathe.

"That's a slam! He slammed her!" Coach is out of his chair and on the mat.

The ref's whistle blows and he calls an injury timeout.

Coach Pettus argues with the ref. "Jerry, you know that was a slam. You were right on top of it."

The ref disagrees. "I didn't see a slam. And Coach, if you've got a question about a call, see me at the scorer's table."

Coach P waives him off and attends to me. Calvin comes over too. They both look worried. "Are you OK, Kayla?" Coach asks.

I remember my proposed response to Jimmy's question an hour ago. I'm even farther from OK now. But that's not what I say.

"I'll be alright. Just need to catch my breath." Calvin hands me a water bottle as I lay on my back. Between Calvin's legs I can see Gray pacing back and forth on his side of the mat. Looking at me. Is he actually smiling?

"Kayla," Coach says, "I think you should default. You're shaken up pretty bad and ..." I don't hear the rest of what he says.

I think about my life. Where I came from, where I came to, and where I am now. I remember the bear. And my father's admonition in my dream. "You've got to face the bear." Well, my bear is smirking at me on the other side of this mat. Ref approaches Coach Pettus and asks, "What are we gonna do?"

"Give me a few more seconds, Jerry," Coach says. Then back to me, "Kayla, there's no shame in a default. You wrestled a great match. And he slammed you pretty hard."

What he's not saying is this. If I default, Gray wins. Just like a pin. I have no idea what the team score is. But I'm not going out this way. I pull myself up into a sitting position, then to my knees. My breath's back to normal. I've felt worse than this before. I look up into Coach's face and smile. "I'm ready." He stares back at me for a second, then helps me to my feet. I didn't notice until now that the crowd had gone quiet. Dead silence. Now, they erupt in applause. The kind of polite applause you hear when an injured player gets carted off the field. Coach grabs my arms and loosens me up. Just says, "Twenty-three seconds," and wiggles his fingers, like he's saying goodbye. I know what he means and I nod.

Turn and run to the center of the mat, staring at Gray the whole way. He looks back at me in shock. Tosses his water bottle and walks back to the center of the mat slowly. Like he doesn't want to be out here anymore. Only have twenty-three seconds until the buzzer goes off. Twenty-three seconds until it's all over for one of us. It's either him or me. There is no other option. I've got to get out from under here. I've gotta escape. The whistle blows.

Nineteen seconds left and I'm still under here. Sweating profusely. How to get out? It's not easy. It's never been easy. But I've done it before, so I can do it again. At least I hope so. There is a lot riding on this—on me. The clock is ticking. Gray has other ideas. He wraps his right arm and around my waist up to my ribcage and squeezes—feels like he's yanking the breath out of my already searing lungs. His calloused left hand feels like a vice around my left wrist. As I push myself off the mat, he rips my left arm off the ground, pushes my upper body toward the space my arm just occupied, and slams my left cheek into the mat. This isn't working. I've got to try something else. I remember Coach's fingers.

Thirteen seconds. I push up to my knees and straighten my back. Out of nowhere, Gray swings his right arm and his bone makes glass-sharp contact with my right cheek and nose. Another cross face. It hurts like hell and he drives my face into my left shoulder in a downward motion. My face hits the floor again and I'm back where I started. I'm running out of time.

Only eight seconds left. It's go time. With my cheek still smashed into the mat, I roll my head until my face points straight down and I can balance on the top of my forehead. I've got to get his fingers, get that arm from around my waist. Four fingers would be ideal, but I'll settle for two. I reach for his hand near my left rib cage and dig for his fingertips. Can't do it. Damn. Wait, I'm under one, now another, and the third finger peels off my waist with the second. That's enough. I'm running out of time. His fingernails dig into the tender pads on my fingertips. But I don't about the pain. Rip his fingers away and the hand and arm follow. One leg up, now the other.

Four seconds. I hang onto his fingers with my right hand. Sorry buddy, I own your fingers now. He's only holding my left wrist with his left hand. His grip still feels like the talons of a raptor, but I'm not worried. I'm getting out of here. I swim my wrist like a Balinese dancer and snap.

That part is always so easy. I'm free. I'm out. I've escaped.

The buzzer goes off and I look to the ref. He's holding up one finger. High in the air. The scoreboard reads 3-2 and just a bunch of zeros on the clock. I glance down to the team score and my jaw drops. Felton 34 - Sheffield 32. Gray tries to slap my hand, but the ref calls him back to shake hands again. Play nice, Rick. Ref raises my hand and I turn to my teammates. Allow myself one fist pump. Just one.

Then I run, feels like I'm soaring, into the mass of my teammates. Hugs, back slaps and congratulations all around. Hollis and Jimmy hoist me to their shoulders for a victory lap around the barn, with the team following. The crowd roars from both the ground level and the rafters above. Faces appear, then disappear again in a blur. Kenna Faye and Sarah. They are beaming. Then my family. Griff sits with them. And the furniture store lady. June has tears in her eyes and Junior cheers like a madman. We stride past the Sheffield team and Rick sits slumped in the corner, his head down. A towel covers his face.

The guys put me down near our bench and the cheering continues. Stefano hands me my sweats. He beams. Most of the people from the rafters have moved to the barn floor. Packed together around the mat. They call to me. I cross the mat toward them. A warm feeling starts in my stomach and spreads throughout my body. Just ahead, outstretched hands and arms reach for me. People call my name. Some folks I know, some I don't know. They want me. Tugging me. Pulling me in to become one with them. I melt into the joyful multitude. I don't want this feeling to end.

CHAPTER THIRTY-THREE: TURN AND FACE
THE STRANGE

But it does end. That good feeling. Sometime about mid-February. Two months ago. In the dead of winter. Like Icarus, I fell to the earth. Took a while to touch down after the buzz of that day. The day of that meet in the barn in the snowstorm. But fell I did. And life, as in high school life, goes on. And on. And on.

After school today, I wander aimlessly to the cafetorium and take a seat near the back. Away from the stage. A middle school drama club is up there reading through a script. I sip my water, eat the rest of my granola bar from lunch and think. Then I think some more. In the middle of my thoughts, deep ones I might add, I glimpse somebody approaching. At first, I don't look up. Until I hear a familiar voice.

"Hi Kayla." It's Mr. Chenoweth. Probably on his way to the vending machine or the fridge in the teacher's lounge or somewhere.

"Hi Mr. C."

"What are you doing in here?"

"Just chilling."

"I mean, why aren't you out enjoying the nice weather?"

Why indeed? "I just felt like sitting here a while. To decompress. Perchance to dream." He smiles at the Shakespeare reference.

"Are you OK? You look a little…down."

"Yeah…I'm…" What am I exactly? Not morbidly sad like I was back in September, but missing… what? My friends? They're still here and still my friends. But there's something about the closeness I felt with all the guys during the wrestling season. Like we were a band of brothers. Going into battle together against guys who wanted to do us harm. But I can't tell him that. What can I say?

"It's like there's…something… something missing. I don't know what I feel."

"Well, you had a lot of excitement during the wrestling season. You guys were celebrities around here. People look at you like some kind of hero."

"No they don't," I reply, but in a friendly way. I like Mr. C.

"No, Kayla, actually they do. Some kids anyway. And some kids around here need a champion. Someone to look up to. Somebody these young girls can be inspired by."

"I don't think that's me."

"Don't sell yourself short, kiddo." I stare off at the stage for a while. They're doing a play version of *The Big Friendly Giant* and some kid stomps around the stage complaining about "snozzcumbers." All the boys on stage laugh hilariously. I expect Mr. C to continue on his mission, but he's still here. Just waiting. Like he's thinking about something.

"So, you're missing something? Maybe your next quest?"

"I don't know."

"Well, I'm just a high school English teacher. But here's what I think. I think you can make your mark around here in more than a wrestling competition."

"How?"

"Well, the way I see it, when you joined the wrestling team, you really found your place in this school. Would you agree?"

"I guess, but…"

"And finding where you belong in high school is not an easy thing. Some kids never do it. But something else happened through your wrestling."

He waits for me to ask. So I do. "What's that?"

"I think you've grown and changed a lot. Give me a synonym for 'grow and change.'" He likes this game.

"Uhhh, transform?"

"Good. Another."

"Evolve?" He spins his finger. I'm supposed to keep going. "Metamorph…

"ose," he offers. "The verb form. And that one is particularly relevant. For you."

"How?"

"Since the beginning of the school year," he says, "you've come out of your cocoon."

"Are you saying I was a caterpillar?" He laughs and shakes his head.

"You reinvented yourself through the wrestling team. But it doesn't mean you have to stop growing and changing."

"I don't know how to play any other sports."

"Did you know how to wrestle a few months ago?"

"Touche."

"But I'm not talking about another sport. I've got something different in mind. Something you'd be very well suited for."

"Like what?"

"I know for a fact that you're a very talented writer."

"I like writing. It's easy. And fun."

"Well, it's not easy for most kids, Kayla." He looks away for a minute. Then looks back at me. Pulls a paper out of the pocket of his beige khakis and hands it to me.

Indiana Writers Guild

Student Short Story Contest

Open to Freshmen and Sophomores Enrolled in Indiana Public Schools

Topic: Imagining your Future - Twenty-five Years From Now

No more than 1200 Words
Submissions Due April 20th
By E-mail: alison@iwg.org
First place prize: Two night stay in the
Indianapolis City Circle Hilton Hotel and
Two passes to the Indianapolis Theater Festival,
June 8-22.

"So what's this?" I ask, playing dumb.

"I think you should enter, Kayla."

"What? The deadline's only ten days away and I can't…"

"Yes, you can. Work on it after school. This weekend. Whenever. You've got time."

"I don't think I…"

"If you've got time to sit in here by yourself, you've got time to write. What do you say?"

"I'll think about it."

"There isn't time to think about it. Just do it. I can help you. Brainstorm ideas. Read your drafts. Whatever. But I'm not going to write it for you."

"I'd never ask you to do that."

"I know you wouldn't. This needs to be

your creative process. You're writing about your future. Only you can control that." I stare down at the pamphlet. A weekend in Indy and theater tickets. I could take Kenna Faye. Cool and cool. But ten days? Is this crazy? Probably. Is it any crazier than stepping out on a wrestling mat? Challenges seem to find me like a moth is attracted to a flame.

"OK. I'm in. But I'll need the whole ten days to write it."

"Not a problem. But if you want me to review it, you'll need to get me your draft by a week from Saturday." I nod. He leaves the pamphlet with me, turns and starts out the door. Didn't he come here to buy something? As if he can read my thoughts he turns around. "Kayla, you won't regret this. It's going to make you think about a challenging subject. Where and how you envision yourself in the future. You'll have fun doing this."

He turns again and this time, he walks out. Seven months ago, I couldn't think of anything but the past. My own past. What I'd lost. Now he wants me to think about the future? How do I get myself into these things? I stand and walk to the door, re-tracing Mr. Chenoweth's steps.

CHAPTER THIRTY-FOUR: IMAGINE ALL THE PEOPLE

This house is a hive of activity. Everybody moving about. Here to there and back again. Out the door and back inside. Over and over. They've got places to go. People to see. Junior walks through this time carrying a baseball bat with his glove stuck on the end. A fishing pole in the other hand. Denise follows him, carrying her jump rope, a kickball and under her arm, the book she just started reading. Geneva holds her baby bunny gently to her chest. All wrapped up in blankets with a tiny hat on its head. I touch her head as she walks by and she smiles up at me. June strides by with a bundt cake in one hand and a casserole in her other. She stops abruptly in front of me, balancing her food. I take the bundt cake when it wobbles in her hand.

"Girl, you need to get changed and all. We got to get movin' here," June says, less exasperated than usual.

"I told you I can't go. I have to finish up my paper today and get it to Mr. Chenoweth."

"Can't it wait till tomorrow?" she asks. "Today's the Chataugua." No idea what this thing is. Some kind of a big town picnic or something. "They only do it once a year and we..."

"I can't go. I gotta get my story done. And it has to be in to him by today."

June's face drops, "But everybody's going to be there. And Arvin and me. We got something..." She looks over at Arvin and he shakes his head. He seems sad too. What did I do? I haven't told them that Hollis invited me to go to the thing with him. Told him I had to write my paper.

"Well, if you get finished up early, ride on over to Yantser's farm. You know where that is?" I nod. "We'll be in the field behind the barn. Till near supper time."

When they finally leave the house, the place is quiet. Eerily so. I grab a Diet Pepsi and walk up to my room. Close the door and walk to my desk. My story stares at me from the screen. I sit and write. At twelve forty-three p.m., I hit print. Put the pages in order, staple them and read to myself.

A mountain of papers on my kidney shaped, thick, glass-top desk leans precariously near the edge. Big sigh. I thought we were doing away with paper years ago. How do half the trees on the planet end up on my desk? I whirl in my ebony ergonomic chair, shove back from my desk, stand and stretch. Another speaking engagement tonight. It's only 5:30 and I'm already exhausted. Guess that's why they invented coffee.

I step as close as I dare to my floor-to-ceiling window and gaze out. I still can't get used to clouds floating underneath me. That's life seventy-two stories above Chicago. A pair of hawks playing in the thermals - swirling in perfect circles up and up—then diving on their unsuspecting prey. We humans aren't that far removed from the animal world—at least not in this town.

Glance north up Lake Shore Drive and follow the thousands of red blinking lights as far as I can see. In the fading light, I can just make out the Bahai Temple in Wilmette. I follow the stretches of sand on Lake Michigan as they dot the shore from the city limit. Finally, the harbors begin.

First Montrose, then Belmont and finally Diversey. No boats this time of year. The harbors always look a bit lonely in the winter. Then the long stretch of North Avenue Beach and the tiny patch of Oak Street Beach - the granddaddy of them all. Just down from Oak Street, Navy Pier juts into the lake - all decked out for Christmas, which is more than three weeks away. Almost looking straight down now, my eyes rest on the river. Pedestrians look like ants walking along the plaza of our building. I close my cobalt blue curtains and check out the batik fabric for a minute. You've come a long way, baby.

A tentative knock. So soft, but enough to pull me back to the present. "Ms. Burbadge, a package just arrived for you - from the UPS guy."

"What's in it, Jenny?"

"I didn't open it. It's marked 'personal and confidential.'"

I furrow my brow as I examine the obviously re-purposed cardboard box. "I almost never get anything personal at the office. Wonder what it is?" Jenny smiles and shrugs. She's an ambitious 25-year-old intern with a bright future ahead of her in the media world. We need more strong women like Jenny at Women's Sports Network. She'll probably be sitting in my chair one day. She passes the package over to me. It's heavier than I imagined - maybe eight to ten pounds. A few items clank inside...

I finish reading and stare at the page, frowning. Can't see my own face, but I know I'm doing it—frowning. It's not right. The paper. It's not me. It's not what I... a light bulb pops up off over my head. I crumple the pages, throw them in the trash can and return to my keyboard.

I sit at my plain wooden desk and stare at the clock as if mesmerized. It's 3:22 p.m., and I've still got a lot of things to do. Organize my stack of papers to grade, for one thing. I made the kids write about King Lear today. Most of them complained about how much they hated it, but I could tell one girl loved the assignment. A girl who hasn't said three words the whole semester. That's the kind of moment that makes teaching high school worthwhile.

I grab my whistle and keys to the wrestling room. Practice starts at 4 and I've got a couple of calls to make. Denise, Junior and I are getting all the cousins together for June's surprise birthday party this weekend. Geneva is driving down from Chicago with her new boyfriend. June will pretend to hate all the fuss, but I know that secretly she loves seeing our boys and the other grandkids. We'll drive down from our little bungalow along the canal in Indianapolis on Saturday morning. It will be great to catch up with the family. Hard to find time during wrestling season.

Since I started coaching at Park Castle High School three years ago, seems like a lot has happened. It took a while for the wrestlers to get used to their first woman coach. But they soon found out that I can be just as hard-nosed as any guy coaching the sport. We've got three girls on the team this year. Not a lot, but it's a start. I grab my wrestling shoes, switch off my light, lock my classroom door and head for the gym.

I read and nod, drop the paper on my desk, write a short e-mail and hit "send". Run downstairs and grab my hooded Felton High sweatshirt. And grab the phone. He picks up on the first ring.

"Hello."

"Hollis, you're still there," I say.

"Course I'm here. I told you I'd wait for you."

"Can you come over and pick me up?"

"I'll be over in five minutes. Bye." Then, just the dial tone. I walk slowly to the front door and   wait.

CHAPTER THIRTY-FIVE: I'M JUST BEGINNING

Hollis drives the direct route to Yantser's farm. No tour through town, no stopping at the mini-mart, no loop through the high school parking lot or trip to the cemetery. It's a lovely spring day and it'd be fun to just ride around, with my elbow out the window, watching the world go by. But I'm a girl on a mission.

As we drive the mile or so out to Yantser's place, Hollis sings along with a song on the radio by a singer named Natasha Bedingfield. Something about blank pages. He's not a great singer, but that's OK.

We begin to pass cars parked along County Road 650 SE. Lots and lots of cars. Mostly trucks, actually, and mostly battered, dented and paint peeling. Farmers' trucks. Working people's trucks. Trucks belonging to our friends and neighbors and classmates and teachers. Trucks backed up along the county road for more than a half-mile before the gravel road leading into Yantser's. I ask Hollis if we shouldn't go back and park. He assures me he knows a secret place.

This must be one gigantic soiree. Or Chautauqua, as June called it. I looked up the term before I started writing. I do tend to procrastinate. Just a touch. Apparently, a Chautauqua was an old-time event that brought entertainment and culture for rural communities, with speakers, teachers, musicians, entertainers, and educators. Who knew these things existed? That they revived these things? And here in Felton? Not me, that's for sure.

Hollis pulls into the farm across the street from the entrance and parks. The only car in an empty lot. He tells me it's his uncle's place and his family has been parking here for ages. We walk across the road and enter the gravel drive. Hollis reaches down and takes my hand. I look down at our joined hands, but say nothing. Just keep walking. Some people walk in, while other families, many with dirty but smiling children, make their way back out from the farm and down the long road to their cars. Many people say "Hello" or "Good afternoon" as they pass. A few know my name.

Everybody knows Hollis. Even those who say nothing still smile at us. No one seems surprised to see us together.

I'm definitely underdressed. While the kids are dressed in overalls and jeans, most of the women wear long, billowing skirts and dresses. Many with spring colors. Flowery prints abound. Not sure if I fall into the adult or kid category. Guess I can be one of the kids for a day.

We walk past the barn, as June instructed. Pretty easy to see where everyone is going. Just behind the barn, still painted with a fading maroon Mail Pouch Tobacco sign, a gentle clover-covered hill spills down into a valley—a big pond (or is it a small lake?) in its center.

Spread out in front of me, maybe one hundred yards down the hill, is a scene that looks familiar. Where have I seen this before? I stop and drink it all in. Suddenly, a memory floods back. First, I get a mental picture, then feel a warmth spreading through my body. One of the best days of my life. A field trip to the Art Institute of Chicago with my sixth grade class. Dad was between projects, so both he and Mom chaperoned.

They were genuinely happy to hang out with the kids. Showed us all their favorite paintings. Mom said that the museum was like an old friend. Familiar, but always full of surprises.

One of the first things we saw that day—you can't miss it really, because it's huge and right when you walk in—was the famous Seurat painting. The enormous *Sunday on La Grande Jatte.* Men, women and children all dressed up, enjoying themselves in a park, on the edge of a lake, on a sun-dappled weekend morning. I look up and the same scene appears before me. Right here. Only these are real people. And they are moving. Moving nearly imperceptibly from up here. But this is no painting; it's real life. With real people. In a real place. And I'm here. We're here. Now. In the moment. We walk down the slope and join the party.

Nearing the crowd, faces begin to appear. They look up as I walk in. Coach sits a few feet off the lake. On a blanket, with Emmy at the corner. An older woman sits with them on a camping chair. Must be Coach's wife sitting beside him on the blanket. He starts to rise and I motion him to stay on the ground. We shake hands all around and the older lady, whom I've never met, pulls me in for a hug. She tells me to come over for fried chicken later. After I find my family. I nod my head, wave at the group and we move on.

As we near the center of the crowd, more and more people greet me by name. Some offer a hand to shake. Some offer picnic food, a chair or a blanket. Some hug me and suggest where I might find my family.

At the far corner of the lake, I spot them. June cuts her bundt cake, while Arvin stands to the side talking to a group of his friends. Junior fishes in the pond with two other boys. They laugh at a boy who drops his pole when a fish bites. Geneva sits one blanket over. Playing dolls with two little blond girls. The other girls have dolls, but Geneva plays with her baby bunny. Denise sits under a nearby tree, reading her book. She looks up as I approach and waves. Sets her book down, says, "Mom?" and points at Hollis and me.

June looks up as she kneels on the blanket. Her face was a mask of concentration as she cut the cake, but a look of joy spreads over her features as she sees us walk in. She stands, walks the few feet to Arvin and whispers in his ear. He takes her hand and they approach us.

"Kayla," June says, surprised. "You made it. Thanks for riding her over, Hollis."

"I waited," Hollis says. "Didn't want Kayla to miss her first Chautaq…this party."

"Well, we're glad you're here," say June. "Both of you. Hollis could you give us a couple of minutes alone? With Kayla?"

He nods and says, "Save your first dance for me?"

"Sure," I say, turning back to June and Arvin. June looks up at Arvin and he nods toward a small grove of trees. Arvin takes my hand in his free one and we walk over. The three of us. Hand in hand. We stop in the shade of the small grove. What is going on here?

"Arvin, you want to?"

Arvin looks first at me, then back at June. "No, why don't you say."

"OK," June begins. She seems really nervous. I've never seen her like this. "We got something we want to ask you. Arvin and me both." She looks up at him and he nods solemnly. "What we want to ask is this. Would you be OK with it if we adopted you? All legal and formal? You're a part of our family now. Part of our community. We want to make it all official."

I stare at them, stunned.

She continues, "Well Kayla, what do you think?"

I look up into their faces. Their tanned, lined, worn faces. Their hopeful faces. I've looked into the future. I don't have to *think*. I know.

I belong.

ACKNOWLEDGEMENTS

I want to recognize the significant contributions of a number of faculty of the University of North Carolina at Charlotte English Department. First, I would like to thank Dr. Elizabeth Gargano, in whose Young Adult Fiction class this novel was begun and nurtured. Then, I would like to thank Dr. Paula Connolly whose British Child Literature class significantly informed my protagonist's reading choices and who first encouraged me to finish this novel as my Master's thesis. Next, I would like to thank Dr. Paula Eckard, whose encouraging words at the initiation of this project provided much needed confidence in my ability to see the book through to completion. I would especially like to thank my thesis advisor, Dr. Mark West, whose insightful constructive advice has proven invaluable throughout this project. I especially appreciate his offering to take this project on in light of his other substantial responsibilities.

I would further like to recognize the invaluable contributions of some of my earliest reviewers, including young adult readers like Lucy and Maggie from the neighborhood and my sons Mason and Arthur who kept me honest with my wrestling portrayals.

I'd like to recognize the artistic talent of my sister Christi Bastnagel for her cover photography and her daughter Betsy, who is the perfect depiction of Kayla on the cover.

Finally, I'd like to thank my editor extraordinaire, personal confidante and partner of many years, Pam Hutson.

Made in the USA
San Bernardino, CA
16 December 2019